Visiting Your
ANCESTRAL TOWN

Walk in the Footsteps of Your Ancestors

F TSTEPS
MEDIA

Library of Congress Cataloging-in-Publication Data
Library of Congress Control Number: 2019900477
ISBN: 978-1-7320382-0-2 (paperback)
ISBN: 978-1-7320382-1-9 (e-book)

Library of Congress subject headings: Ancestry Travel, Family History, Family History Vacations, Genealogy, Genealogy Vacation, Family Heritage Travel, Travel, Travel Guidebook

*For my parents, who instilled in me
a love of family and exploration.*

*And for all those ancestors of mine, who came from such
interesting places that I now get to explore.*

Table of Contents

A Few Words about the Third Edition

I guess I just can't get enough of writing about ancestral towns, so here I go for a third time. New ideas and techniques make this an ever-changing hobby to keep up with!

The third edition includes a couple of new chapters on topics I've become passionate about. One is using DNA for genealogy research—the more I get into it, the more fun I have. But on the flip side, I keep hearing people getting wound up when their ethnicity estimates don't match what they know about their heritage. DNA research is so valuable—and so much more than those ethnicity estimates. The new chapter provides a few tips as a starter guide to help you incorporate DNA into your genealogy research and start making the most of this powerful tool.

Another new chapter is on exploring the social history of your ancestors—what they ate, how they lived—deepening your understanding of their lives so they're not just names on a page. Traveling to an ancestral town is one of the very best ways to embrace the culture of your ancestors.

In this edition and previous editions, I've illustrated my research and travel tips with stories. But I have so many more stories than the ones I've been able to include. Therefore, at the end of each chapter, I've added a section called "In Their Footsteps"—adapted from past blog posts I have written—so that I could include a few more of my favorite stories and adventures.

Go forth and seek out your roots!

Chapter 1

Why Visit an Ancestral Town?

Visiting with the Kram family of Kassel (Velykokomarivka), Ukraine

What's Your Reason?

Black sheep ancestors. Rumors of stolen passports and stowaways. That awkward silence at the dinner table when a particular family story comes up that no one wants to talk about. Trying to understand your love of schnitzel when you've never been to Germany.

Seeking out your ancestors and visiting the places where they lived is a deeply personal journey. What you find may help you know yourself a little better. It may help you understand your love for certain foods or languages. It may deepen your sense of connection with family members that have gone before you. It may surprise you.

Whatever your reason, walking in the footsteps of your ancestors is an unforgettable experience.

Family memoirs and stories

Haven't we all heard our parents tell stories like: "Don't complain about walking to school, young lady. When I was your age, I'd milked the cows and fed the chickens before walking four miles to school."

But even as I rolled my eyes, my parents' and grandparents' stories gave me an intriguing glimpse into the world they grew up in that is so different from my world of the internet and smartphones and Facebook. Their stories made me want to see the places they talked about.

My mother grew up in the town of Lehr, North Dakota, in the 1920s and '30s. Many of the memories of her youth grew fuzzier for her over time, but never the stories of the annual camp meetings her church held at the nearby Lehr Tabernacle. Even when she was in her eighties, her face would light up as she re-experienced the delight she and her friends had searching the straw floor for coins that had dropped from people's pockets. And then her stories would shift into her young adulthood, when she and her friends would walk into the prairie hills beyond the tabernacle, playing guitars and singing gospel songs, laughing, and, of course, flirting with the young men.

Although I heard the stories of the camp meetings all my life and we visited my grandparents in Lehr throughout my childhood, I had never seen the tabernacle until I was an adult and took my mom to Lehr for the town's 100th anniversary. After a weekend of parades and church suppers, the final event of the celebration was a service in the tabernacle.

I was surprised to discover the tabernacle was so close to town, at the end of the street where my mother had lived and just across the county road. It was a surprise to see what a huge complex it was, with a separate kitchen building, dorms, washrooms, and a cabin for the visiting pastor, all in addition to the main tabernacle building. Seeing this for myself suddenly made my mom's stories make sense; how so many people could have come to the camp meetings from neighboring towns, and even the next state, and stayed for a whole week.

Seeing the familiar places opened the doors to new memories my mother had never shared before. "That field is where everyone would come and camp out. And I remember all of us sharing a cup to drink water from this pump," she explained, pointing to each location.

But my biggest revelation came during the service itself. My parents had faithfully taken me to church each Sunday when I was growing up. Even as a child I'd loved the music and singing and had never understood how my mother could dutifully stand and hold the hymn book each service but never sing along. She appeared to be completely unmoved by the music.

But in the tabernacle on that Sunday morning in Lehr, the first song was an old gospel hymn, "When We All Get to Heaven." To my surprise, my mom sang out loudly and clearly, never even looking at the hymn book. After all these years, she still knew the words by heart.

When I asked her about it after the service, she said in her usual blunt fashion, "I've never liked those Presbyterian hymns, but I like the old evangelical gospel music!"

Sometimes the memories that are the most meaningful, the most important keys to understanding your family, lie below the surface and need the right trigger to come out. Sometimes you have to dig a little and ask some questions to learn more about your family. By visiting and experiencing her hometown through her eyes, I learned about my mother's love of music (at least some types of music) that I'd never guessed.

Visiting towns of more distant ancestors

The visit to Lehr had a very personal connection for me because of my mother's stories. But I've also visited the towns of more distant ancestors, hoping for a feeling of connection by walking in their footsteps, by seeing the places where they once lived but chose to leave.

When I went to Hoffnungstal (Nadezhdivka in Ukrainian), a German village in Ukraine, I didn't expect much. From previous visitors, I'd learned the village had been destroyed. I would not get to see the house where my grandfather grew up or the church where he was confirmed. Even the cemetery had been destroyed, so I wouldn't find my family's graves.

But even without those tangible family landmarks, I felt a sense of awe in seeing the valley as my great-great-grandparents Peter and Katharina Schott probably first saw it. They were among the earliest settlers, and when they arrived, there would have been few houses. As I stood on the cemetery hill, knowing that somewhere beneath my feet lay the bodies of those great-great-grandparents and dozens of other family members, I felt like I was seeing the lush, green valley with their eyes. I felt the sense of hope they must have felt that caused the village to be named Hoffnungstal (Hope Valley in English). I felt their sense of promise as they started a new life for their young family far away from their own parents and grandparents. And perhaps this same sense of hope and promise later caused my grandfather to leave there and come to America.

Traveling a road less traveled

Visiting an ancestral town can offer a unique travel experience far different than the typical tourist destinations. This gives you the opportunity to see a more remote location and connect with real people living there, rather than just tour guides and hotel clerks. (Unless, of course, your family came from a town that now happens to be a popular tourist destination. But that's not the case for most of us.)

A group of us from a genealogy organization I belong to traveled together to Ukraine to visit our ancestral towns. My friend Gayla was on a mission to photograph every house in her town of Neu Freudental (Marynivka in Ukrainian). The rest of us were just killing time until she was done with her photography. So we wandered into the town's small grocery store, just one long counter and a few shelves, searching for ice cream on what had become a warm September day.

As we purchased our ice cream, I realized this might be my chance to get some extra batteries for my camera. We were directed to the next building, the town's general store, which we would never have recognized as there was no sign on the building. We spent a fascinating half hour poking through the odd selection of merchandise—socks

4

lying next to nail scissors on the crowded counter; dresses hanging on the wall above the bags of cement for sale. But I bought my batteries and, at the same time, got a glimpse of the essential goods found in a general store in a small Ukrainian village.

Even more memorable was another friend's ancestral town, Kassel (Velykokomarivka in Ukrainian). We stopped to see a local family, one of the few remaining that still had ethnic German connections. (Most of the ethnic Germans left these villages in the 1940s.) The family insisted we come in and have lunch with them.

Afraid we were straining their obviously limited financial resources, we insisted on sharing the food we'd brought along. In the one-room home, lived in by three generations of this family, they pulled up the table next to the bed and brought in a bench from the yard outside to give us all a place to sit.

As we shared food and vodka, we also shared stories of our lives— ours in America and theirs in Ukraine. A daughter had moved back to this village to care for her elderly parents but was concerned about how hard it was to find work outside the cities. Then her face lit up as she mentioned her upcoming wedding. While their lives and homes were nothing like our own, their joys and cares were not that different.

Researching your family

You may want to visit an ancestral town to do more research on your family. Despite the growth of genealogy information on the internet, there are many thousands, probably millions, of old documents *not* on the internet that may be available locally. Talking to people in the town hall, church, or museum in your ancestral town, or at a local archive that specializes in information about your town, may bring insights that you would never get from sitting at your computer thousands of miles away. When my cousin visited the town of Landau, Germany, local residents pointed him in the direction of new information that became a breakthrough in his research.

Of course, the jackpot here is if you actually find something new.

I'll have to admit my research in my ancestral lands hasn't given me that "Eureka!" moment, though it has given me some important clues. And having the chance to handle 17th century documents in an archive or discuss the history of an area with a local expert has made for some interesting travel experiences.

On one trip to Germany, I decided to do some research in Wiesbaden. Through a German friend and by finding the archive's website, I discovered the branch of the archive (located in a nondescript residential area) that would help me find information about my ancestors. I was able to verify that I didn't need an appointment for a research visit.

After putting everything but a pen and pad of paper into a locker, I presented myself to the collections desk where they helped me request records through their computer system. Then I stationed myself at a table until one of the archive workers wheeled up a cart stacked with documents, delivering them from the depths of wherever they are kept to me and other waiting researchers.

Although my research that day mostly helped me find where my ancestors weren't, I was a bit in awe at being able to walk in off the street and handle documents from the 1600s, some with the original wax seal still (barely) attached. I read through tax lists and crop lists (which showed lists of village residents). I even found an interesting document in which a Schott widow begged the local count to excuse her from paying taxes because, she argued, her husband had worked hard in the count's service yet never made a penny. She even scolded the count a bit. I was sorry I couldn't find a relationship to me—she sounded spunky and interesting, and I would have loved to claim her as a many-times great-grandmother.

And in the end, this research trip did pay off. Although I left disappointed, it did make me question if I had the right village since none of my family names showed up in the records I'd searched. Sure enough, several years later, I found out my family actually had lived in a different town with a similar name.

Although the research only helped me indirectly, the experience of handling original documents was awesome. Even an apparent dead end can be part of the adventure.

What Will I Experience in My Ancestral Town?

I'm a Type A "make a plan" sort of person. Except when I travel. Then I love to leave space in my plans to pursue any new whims or ideas that come to me.

When traveling to ancestral towns, I'm a firm believer that making some plans in advance increases your chances of having a meaningful experience connecting with your ancestors' lives. But I'm an equally firm believer in leaving some space in my plans so I can experience whatever unfolds, leading me to serendipitous, interesting encounters I could never have orchestrated.

Planning a little or a lot

On my first trip to Germany in my 20s, I was content just to be in the same country where my ancestors had lived. I had no idea what town they'd come from and didn't care. Although I didn't speak enough German at the time to understand what was being said, the cadence of the language was familiar to my ears from hearing it as a child and gave me a sense of familiarity. The smell of the sausage and various dough dishes (dumplings, spätzle) weren't exactly the same as my mother had cooked but were familiar enough that I dove into everything on my plate while my fellow travelers were still timidly poking at their food. Just the realization that the surroundings felt comfortable, even though I'd traveled thousands of miles to a different culture, was enough to make that trip a success for me.

On a later trip, I'd done more research and knew some of the towns where my ancestors had lived. But I still didn't do much more preparation than finding the location on the map. Most of my ancestral villages are small, so once I located them and drove through once, there wasn't much more to see. I visited cemeteries, but most cemeteries in Germany are recycled every 30 years, so I couldn't find any graves of my direct ancestors (who had all left Germany by the early 1800s). I looked at the locked churches and even bought a pastry in one local bakery. But I left without interacting with anyone. It was interesting but not an especially meaningful visit for me.

By contrast, several years ago I visited the town of Ober-Gleen, Germany. For this trip, I did quite a bit of preparation, including making plans to spend the day with the owner of a small art gallery in the town. Someone from the town hall, which I'd contacted via their website, had put me in touch with him because he had an interest in local history. I spent a fabulous day with Herr Bloemers, who showed me around the museum in the neighboring town, shared local history, and gave me some insights into why my ancestor might have left. He had a key to the church, so I got to tour that and even saw the baptismal font where my ancestors were probably baptized. I stayed overnight at a B and B in the next town and ate some of the best spätzle of my life. We had afternoon cake and coffee in the courtyard of his small art gallery, and he told me lively stories about some of his experiences working all over the world for a luxury hotel chain.

It was a fabulous day with an interesting guide and new insights into my ancestors—all because I did a little planning.

Serendipitous experiences

On a trip to Ukraine, I thought I'd prepared thoroughly. I had a map of the village from the time period my ancestors had lived there. I highlighted all the homes with family names and figured out how each related to my family. (Some were the houses of cousins rather than my direct line.)

But the most interesting part of this visit had nothing to do with my planning. It came from meeting Nadia, the vice principal of the school. She showed a group of us around the school (interrupting the classes to the children's delight and the teachers' irritation) and told us its history, and then showed us around the village and to some of the homes I'd highlighted on my map. From hearing the school's history, I realized my great-grandparents had probably gone to school in this very building. Nadia insisted I sit in one of the desks, just like my great-grandparents had.

On a trip to Germany, I'd arranged to meet Friedrich, a distant cousin. He was such a distant cousin that, when I first emailed him, I wasn't even sure how we were related. I only knew there was a connection because my friend and fellow researcher Dale had assured me of it.

Friedrich immediately invited me to stay with him and his wife. This felt a bit odd since I didn't know them at all. But since Dale knew them, I figured it would be okay for one night at least. Then I would continue on with my travel plans, which mostly involved visiting tourist sights—castles and museums.

Friedrich and Ute were so welcoming that I ended up staying with them for three nights instead of just one. They immediately invited me back the following weekend for a family birthday celebration and again later that month to visit a local wine festival. Then they said, "So what other relatives are you planning to visit?"

I hadn't known others even existed. Friedrich insisted on contacting relatives all over Germany to make plans for me to visit them. Instead of the simple tourist month I'd planned, I ended up meeting many new relatives, several of whom I still regularly communicate with more than 17 years later. I missed some of the tour book sights I'd planned on visiting but saw others through the eyes of a local, who also happened to be a distant cousin.

I could never have planned for nor predicted this experience. The personal connections I made gave much more meaning to my search for my family history. The search became more about connecting with people rather than just places.

Disappointments

Of course, travel also brings uncertainty. There is bad weather or missed connections or incorrect information or bad timing. Any of these may cause you to miss something you'd hoped to see. As a regular tourist, that can be frustrating. But on a once-in-a-lifetime trip to visit an ancestral town, these disappointments may feel devastating. Fortunately, the types of problems that can completely derail a trip are rare.

But sometimes disappointment comes when a place that should be meaningful and full of family history has changed too much. I look at the now lonely hillside in North Dakota where my grandfather's farm once stood and where my father grew up. Many buildings are gone, so I have a hard time visualizing the big white house built by my father's uncle, the farmyard bustling with chickens, or the large red barn that all have been described to me.

Where was the barn in relation to the house? And how did my parents manage to "borrow" my grandfather's car out of the barn late at night, pushing it down the hill without starting it (which might wake him up) to get it down to the road? Then, how did they manage the process in reverse at the end of the date to return my grandfather's car and switch back to my dad's?

I've always loved that story because it shows a mischievous side of my parents in their youth that I never saw in them. But the current bare hillside doesn't help me visualize it any better than if I'd just stayed home in Seattle.

What will it be like to visit an ancestral town?

Every trip and set of experiences are unique. Hopefully, your trip will avoid the disappointing moments and allow you to experience something that you would never have expected while sitting at home in front of your computer planning your trip.

Located in the vineyards outside of Osthofen, this apparently was the scene of much post-grape-harvest partying in earlier years.

In Their Footsteps

Welcome Back to Osthofen
(Original blog post: September 15, 2016)

From the very first email, I felt my ancestral town of Osthofen reaching out to welcome me. The email was, of course, not from the town itself but from my guide for the day, Ursula Feile from the tourist office. Her cheery note—"We're so excited you're visiting the town of your ancestors. We'll show you around and drink wine"—immediately drew me in.

The little church

When I arrived in Osthofen, she greeted me with "I have something special planned." Our first stop was a small coffee shop—which also happened to be my ancestors' church. In the 1700s and early 1800s, Ost-hofen had two churches. The large, impressive, stained-glass-windows and frescos-on-the-wall church on the hill overlooking the town was the home of the larger Reform congregation. The Lutheran church (where my Schott family attended) was smaller and plainer, dark wood and white walls, occupying a street corner in the center of town.

Today, the "little church" has been renovated. The top floor is used for worship services in winter, while the ground floor serves as a coffee shop that sells fair trade goods to raise money for projects to alleviate poverty in Africa. I felt so proud. Not only is my ancestors' church still in use, but it practices the social mission of the Church by following Jesus's command to love your neighbor wherever they are. Wow.

It's all about the wine

Wine is an important part of Osthofen's culture—the town is surrounded by vineyards. So the natural next event was hiking through the vineyards, or the Weinberge. I understood Ursula's concern that I wear good shoes for our walk, but it was a bit of a surprise to find that we were actually hiking to the next village. I thought the discussion of nearby Mühlheim was about history, not destination. (Clearly, I needed to work on my German language skills.) But the short hike provided beautiful views and a visit to a centuries-old mill, now the home of one of Ursula's friends.

Ursula had gathered a group of local guides for dinner, all passionate about local history and interested in my journey to seek out my ancestors. They told me about the history of the town; I told them about the Schott family's adventures traveling to Galicia (now western Ukraine) and the Black Sea area after they'd left Osthofen. The restaurant was beautiful with an interesting upscale menu, but was located in a former stable with a soaring stone-vaulted ceiling.

After dinner, we went to a small wine garden, open only a couple of nights per week. It looked more like a big family party than a public place. I would have felt like I was intruding if I'd walked in on my own. But the owners loved my story about seeking out my roots and poured me some wine.

A visit to the big, ornate church on the hill and a personalized tour of the Heimatmuseum (the local area museum) the next morning helped me learn more about how people had lived in Osthofen for centuries. But simply walking through the town with Ursula was almost more special.

She had a gift for relating what we saw to my ancestors' time. She helped me see beyond the modern facade to see the lines of a small typical home in the 18th century. Her descriptions brought blocks of stone and wire fencing along a creek-side walkway to life with scenes of the village women gathering to do their wash and share the daily news.

Finding Susanna

As a genealogist, the most special moment was a trip to the cemetery. I've wandered many cemeteries in search of my ancestors' final resting places. For my grandparents and a couple of great-grandparents in the Dakotas, this was a simple search. But cemeteries in Germany, Ukraine, and Hungary have been a disappointment. German cemeteries in Ukraine and Hungary have mostly been destroyed. Cemeteries in Germany recycle their graves, and you rarely find any older than 35 years.

When Ursula said she had a Schott grave to show me, I didn't hold out much hope. There was another Schott family in Osthofen, larger than mine and connected to the larger Reform congregation. Any Schott graves were likely to belong to them. When she pointed out the partially overgrown stone of Susanna Schott, born 1809—the year my three-times great-grandparents Philipp Jakob and Maria Dorothea (Finger) Schott left Osthofen—I dutifully took a photo, but without much enthusiasm.

But when I compared the photo to my family tree, I discovered that Susanna is related to me not once, but twice! She's my first cousin four times removed because her grandparents Johann Jacob and Anna Margaretha (Lacker) Finger are my four-times great-grandparents. She's also my second cousin four times removed because her great-grandparents Michael and Maria Elisabetha (Reichert) Schott are my five-times great grandparents.

There is still a little part of me, a little trace of my family history, in Osthofen after all.

Captivated by Osthofen

Osthofen is a modern German town, a bedroom community of Worms with an industrial area on the edge of town that no doubt provides employment for much of the population. Its surrounding vineyards give it a pleasant setting, but it doesn't have the storybook, postcard-perfect charm of many German villages I've seen.

But on this visit, Osthofen captivated me. Unlike previous visits, in which I'd wandered the streets on my own, hoping to feel the lingering presence of family ghosts, this time I felt the warmth of the town reach out to me. I could picture Maria Dorothea, and her mother Anna Margaretha before her, gathered at the river washing clothes. I could imagine them leaving their small house and walking to the church for worship each Sunday.

I felt the camaraderie with my new-found friends as local wine fueled an animated discussion of the town's heritage. And in finding Susanna's grave, I found that a little piece of my family remains anchored to the town, despite the wandering of Philipp Jakob and Maria Dorothea as they migrated eastward.

My feet have walked in the path of generations of Schotts and Fingers, and I have been welcomed back after centuries of family wandering. It felt good to be welcomed home.

Chapter 2

Discovering Your Ancestral Town

Found it! This town in Poland was tricky to locate.

Getting Started

The first step in visiting a place where your family has roots is simply to discover where your ancestors came from—the country or town where they were born, had children, lived, and died. That may be easy and common knowledge in your family. But in most cases, it requires doing some research. Knowing basic genealogical research methods is crucial to truly discovering your family roots.

Even if you think you already know where your roots are, doing the research might lead to some surprises. After growing up firm in the knowledge that my family was German (my parents spoke German; my mother cooked German food), it was a big surprise when I discovered a book that showed my grandparents had been born in "South Russia," which is now Ukraine. This seeming contradiction is what spurred my interest in finding out more and caused me to dive headfirst into learning about my family history.

The examples in this book feature the areas where I have personally done most of my research—the United States, Germany, and Eastern Europe. But genealogy principles and many of the resources are the same, so wherever your family roots are, this book should be helpful in seeking out your heritage.

What do you already know?

The best place to start is with what you already know about your family. Of course, some family situations are complicated. You may not know much because there may be missing links and family mysteries that were never talked about. Solving these mysteries may be the reason you're starting this research in the first place.

But even if your knowledge is limited, the best foundation to build on is the family information you already know. Who are your parents? Your siblings? Your grandparents, aunts and uncles, and cousins? Do you know when and where they were born or married or died?

Write it all down and document how you know this information (more about documenting sources a little bit later). Even if there are lots of gaps in your information, this gives you a foundation to build on as you start your journey into family history.

Choosing genealogy software

As you build up your collection of genealogy data, you'll need a way to keep track of it all. This used to be simple—the two choices were paper and a limited set of PC- or Mac-based software programs. Now the selection is dizzying and includes online options and apps for tablets and smartphones.

To wade through all the choices, consider the following:
- Determine the features you need. I'd suggest making a list of a few features most important to you to compare your options.

Considerations include: How easily does the software allow you to enter family information? Do you want the ability to create a family history book or website? Does it allow you to easily add media files (photos, videos, etc.) to individuals in your tree and tag the source of the information? Does it provide flexible options to report on your family data (tree format, report format, etc.)? Does it track genealogy DNA results?

- Determine the device(s) you will use most often for your genealogy. They may include your laptop, tablet, or smartphone. Does the software synch or provide access where you need it to?

These sources may help you identify your software options:
- Top Ten Reviews does an annual comparison of the top software programs: https://www.toptenreviews.com/software/home/best-genealogy-software.
- Cyndi's List provides links for mobile device options, genealogy software, and online genealogy software, but it doesn't include comparisons of the different options: www.cyndislist.com/mobile; www.cyndislist.com/software/genealogy; www.cyndislist.com/software/online-family-trees.
- Dick Eastman is an authoritative voice on genealogy technology and blogs about software and genealogy apps for tablets and smartphones at: http://blog.eogn.com/category/software.

I would be cautious about using an online family tree tool as your only genealogy database. Some sites that offer this service charge a subscription fee. Do you want to be trapped forever into subscribing because all of your precious genealogy data is there? What if the site crashes or goes out of business? (Admittedly, this is unlikely with some of the largest genealogy providers, but it's still something to keep in mind.)

On the other hand, it can also be dangerous for your only genealogy database to be on your laptop, as that can crash or be stolen. Backing up your data is vital, as well as storing your backup drive separately from your computer to prevent both from being stolen. Having your data online, in addition to on your laptop, or backing up your data in the cloud (internet) is crucial for protecting the valuable family data on your laptop.

Personally, I have my main genealogy database (using Family Tree Maker software) on my laptop, the device that is most comfortable for me to use to enter data and to scan and attach photos and documents. I also have my family tree loaded to an online website (the Black Sea German Research site, which is free and focused on my specific area of research). This makes it easy for me to connect with other researchers and to access my genealogy information using my smartphone wherever I am.

The only slight disadvantage to my approach is when I'm talking with a newly discovered relative, I can't immediately enter their data using my ever-present smartphone. Even though I've started to look into getting an app for my smartphone, I recognize that wrestling with software may not be the best method for jotting down data during an interview. ("Wait, where was your grandfather born again? Just a minute, let me tab over to that field. His father? Wait, wait, I need to click on a different page. Just a sec, my connection seems to be slow right now.")

I've found that recording a conversation or jotting down notes on my phone's notes app or even on paper has actually worked quite well for me, even without a genealogy app on my smartphone.

What does your family know?

Now it's time to expand your research by interviewing your family members—parents, grandparents, aunts, uncles, cousins. Ask everybody. Ask anyone who will sit still for a moment to tell you what they know or have heard about your family.

Don't be shy. Call Great-Aunt Martha even if no one in the family has spoken with her in a decade. In fact, *especially* call Great-Aunt Martha and any other older relatives. They often have a fount of knowledge, including family legends, stories of family black sheep, and little tidbits of information that you will never be able to find in any official source such as vital records or church records.

I spent a recent Christmas in my dad's hometown. My cousin invited an older couple over for coffee so I could talk with Jim about the times he worked for my grandfather as a teen and also find out what he knew about my dad and uncle's local business ventures in the 1940s.

Jim laughed when he got the invitation. "We always used to want to talk with the old people about how things used to be. And now I am the old people!" But he had several anecdotes about my grandfather hiring him and other teens to clear rocks from the fields and paying them in cigarettes. He knew some great background information about all the car dealerships in the area, which helped me better understand my dad and uncle starting a new car dealership in their small hometown of Kulm, North Dakota, and he even remembered some of my dad's customers.

And (not to be morbid) don't wait to interview your older relatives. I'll always regret not talking with my Aunt Edna, who was interested in our family history and knew all sorts of family stories from her mother (my grandmother), who died when I was only 3 years old. Aunt Edna was always such a ball of energy; I could never imagine a time she wouldn't be around. She lived nearby, so it was easy to put it off, thinking, "Oh, I can easily run over there one day and ask her a few questions." But before I got around to it, Aunt Edna died suddenly of a heart attack at age 77.

Don't wait.

Interviewing and using family legends to further your research

If your family member is comfortable with this, record your interview as that will let you focus on the conversation, rather than on taking notes or fumbling with your genealogy software. Record your conversation using your smartphone, voice recorder, or video.

If the person you are interviewing is relaxed and feels like they're just having a conversation with you, they're much more likely to remember interesting details than if they feel pressured by you recording each detail in your computer or smartphone. A strict interview format may make them try so hard to answer your questions that they actually won't remember as much as if they'd just been free to reminisce.

Some people will be naturals—you can ask a couple of open-ended questions, and they'll eagerly spill out hours of interesting family information and memories. But others will need a bit more prompting. It's good to come prepared with a list of questions and topics you want to cover. See the appendix for a list of some questions you might ask.

When you talk to family members, ask them what they know or remember about their parents, aunts and uncles, and grandparents. Ask them if they know the dates their family members were born, married, or died. Ask them where they lived, when they moved, what they did for a living, what they ate, and what their daily lives were like. Ask them if they have any photos, as these can provide useful clues about family connections. Armed only with a formal family photo belonging to her great-aunt and the family legend that in her great-grandfather's family, "all the girls stayed in Sweden and all the boys came to America," a friend of mine did a letter-writing campaign to all the members of the Lilja family in a town in Nebraska to identify the connections between the Lilja family in the photo and her Peterson family.

Even if a family member doesn't remember specific names and dates, don't give up. A fellow genealogist tells the story of how he tried in vain to get names and dates by showing a photo to an elderly family member, but she didn't remember many of them. But when he said, "You all look very sad in this photo. What was happening?" she opened up with the story of how her father and uncles had been arrested by the Soviets. They were let out of prison long enough for a family funeral (the scene of the photo) but were executed soon afterward. By knowing the story of what was happening, he was able to find arrest records for these men. That gave him the dates and many of the names to fill in the blanks that he was looking for—as well as a deeper understanding of the tragedy his family had experienced.

Ask your family members if they know if anyone else in the family has ever done genealogy research in the past. My Netz family research started out with an extensive foundation because a distant aunt had once done research and sent it to my cousin, who was more than willing to get rid of it by giving it to me when I asked.

Encourage them to talk about unproven family legends and rumors. Not only will these help you get to know your ancestors as real people, rather than just as names and dates, but these legends can also give you important clues that could help your research.

Two family legends helped me find my grandfather's name on a ship's passenger list. One rumor, which was voiced in our family over and over again, was that my grandfather had been a stowaway on a ship to the U.S. The second rumor, the source of which I don't remember, was that my grandfather had used his married brother-in-law's passport to come to the U.S. because it allowed him to escape military conscription in Russia.

There were holes in both of these stories. About three-fourths of the German-Russian researchers I know have family stories about their immigrant ancestors being stowaways, and I don't think any of them have proven to be true. And although my grandfather's brother-in-law was married, that wouldn't necessarily have exempted him from military service in early 1900s Russia, so using the brother-in-law's passport would not have helped my grandfather avoid military conscription. Also, the U.S. didn't require a passport to enter in 1905 when my grandfather arrived.

So I set out to find his passenger list and disprove the prevalent stowaway rumor. And yet, I couldn't find it anywhere. Peter Schott was not on any passenger list index I could find. The shipping line that he referenced on his Declaration of Intent (one step in the process of becoming a citizen) had a number of ships arriving in the U.S., but none seemed to have arrived in the main port of New York at the right time to match when he got to North Dakota. I started to wonder if he'd purposely provided misleading information and maybe the stowaway legend was true after all.

On a whim, I decided to look for his brother-in-law, Jakob Schuldheisz. I knew Jakob came to the U.S., so I expected to find him in the passenger list index and didn't expect that would help my search for my grandfather Peter. And sure enough, I found Jakob on the index right away. Oddly, it showed him arriving on a ship that was earlier than when I knew he had immigrated. But it was exactly the same time that my grandfather had arrived. I decided to check it out.

The microfilm of the passenger list for this ship from Bremen to Baltimore simultaneously answered my question and created a new one that I haven't solved to this day. In different writing than the original passenger list, the name Schuldheisz had been converted to Schott by scratching out "heisz," turning the *u* to an *o*, and crossing the *ld* to make it look like *tt*. Jakob had been scratched out and changed to Peter, and his contacts in the U.S. had been changed from "friends Fred and Christ Schott in North Dakota" to "bro Fred and Christ Schott in North Dakota." It clearly looked like Jakob Schuldheisz had originally been written then later changed to Peter Schott. This was my grandfather's passenger list entry, but it had been indexed under the original name of Jakob Schuldheisz, which is the reason I couldn't find my grandfather in the index.

Without knowing the rumor about the passport, I would never have looked for Jakob Schuldheisz and would never have proven that my grandfather wasn't a stowaway. At the same time, it creates a mystery I may never solve. Why did my grandfather use his brother-in-law's name on the passenger list? (Even if he used Jakob's passport to get out of Russia, surely there wouldn't have been any danger of getting caught by the Russian government when he was boarding the ship in Germany.) When and why did the passenger list get corrected? Did he accidentally give himself away that his name wasn't Jakob, which forced it to be corrected? Or did he simply want to set the record straight? And was the loan of the passport the reason that Jakob and family didn't come to the U.S. for another six years? (I can't imagine how difficult it must have been to convince the Russian government in 1905, "Woops, I lost my passport and need a new one.")

I may never know the answers to these questions, unless I can find someone who knows another family legend.

Documenting Your Research

Every fact you put into your family tree should be documented with the source of the information. Yes, I really mean every one of them.

When you start your research, it's easy to think, "Oh, those are my cousins; I know I got all that information from Uncle Patrick." Or, "This book on Kilkenny has so much information; I'll know that anything I have recorded about Kilkenny came from this book."

But as you expand your research into vital records and church records and other researchers' family trees, you'll start to discover conflicting information. Did my Schott family come from: (A) Ludwigsburg, Germany (as listed in a book of family origin data that was compiled 130 years after the family arrived in Russia); or (B) Osthofen, Germany (as listed in the Osthofen church records)? Were my Billigmeier great-great-great-grandparents married in: (A) 1811 (information sent to me by one researcher); (B) 1812 (the Gräfenhausen, Germany, church records); or (C) 1814 (sent to me by another researcher)? (The answer in both these cases is B, because those are original records, recording the event closest in time to when it happened.)

Knowing your sources enables you to sort out the data that is most likely to be correct when you have conflicting information. Having bad data can lead you astray in your genealogy . . . and lead you to the wrong place if you're planning a trip to visit an ancestral town. If you don't know your sources, it's impossible to figure out which piece of conflicting information is more reliable.

A few tips in documenting your sources include:

- Document everything, even facts you personally know. The source on my parents' birth dates is "Carolyn Schott, personal knowledge" since I know these because we celebrated them each year. Though it's still best to also corroborate these facts with church or civil records.

- Document even informal conversations with relatives or other researchers that provide family data. Include their name and the date of the conversation, email message, Christmas card, etc. The source in my family tree for several recent babies in the family is "Per birth announcement by [mom's name] on Facebook on [date]."

- Make copies (digital or paper) of documents (such as census records or church records) in which you find information, in addition to noting the reference information (e.g., document name and page number). Most genealogy software allows you to attach images to individuals, which you can use to attach JPGs or PDFs of the documentation as well as photos. Sometimes, as you learn more about your family, there will be clues in the original document that you didn't notice at first, and you'll want to look at it later.

- Document where you've looked for information, even if you don't find anything. This will prevent you from covering the same ground over again later. I can't tell you how many times I've looked at an ancestor in my family tree and thought, "I should really go find her birth date," only to realize when I'm looking at the relevant church record that I've already looked at it multiple times before—and it still doesn't have the piece of information I'm looking for. I need to expand my research to new sources.

- Make a note of and document even the crazy family stories.

While they may not be accurate, they can be great clues to help you find the real facts. (Just make sure you don't record them as fact until you verify that the crazy story really happened.)

For the ultimate guide in citing your sources, the book *Evidence Explained*, by Elizabeth Shown Mills, describes in detail how to record them, as well as an overview of how to evaluate the reliability of these sources.

When evaluating sources of conflicting data to determine which source is most reliable, some of the factors to consider include:

- Is the source of your information an original record (or an actual image of the original)? Or is it a derivative? Derivative sources include transcriptions, translations, or data extracted from original records. These processes leave room for error, so they are less reliable.

- Did the person supplying the information have first-hand knowledge of the event? A parent's information on the birth date of a child is more likely to be correct than a distant relative reporting on the birth.

- How near in time to the event was it recorded? A marriage recorded in a town's church records (which would usually happen at the same time as the actual event) is more reliable than a marriage date shown in a census that was recorded 40 years later.

- Are there any biases or external conditions that would affect the accuracy of the information? Children are frequently listed on ship passenger lists as younger than they actually were so they could pay a lower fare. For my Black Sea Germans, a valuable source of family data is the forms filled out by families in the 1940s when they were being repatriated from Russia to Germany and had to prove their German ethnicity by documenting their ancestors. But since they were being forced to abandon their homes and most of their possessions, it's highly likely they were distressed enough not to fill out every date exactly right.

All of this may sound complicated, but it's really just common sense. Write down where you got your information so you can figure out what is most likely to be accurate—an official record or the unreliable memory of an elderly relative recalling events that happened 80 years before.

Expanding Your Research

In parallel with talking to your family members, you'll probably want to dive into more resources to start expanding your research. Some of these include:

- **Online sources:** There has been an explosion in the last five to ten years of genealogy information online, as well as numerous websites devoted to this popular hobby. Online sources of information can include original records (images or extracts of the data in the records), family trees that other researchers have compiled, and numerous sites that specialize in specific types of records or types of research.

- **Vital records:** These are official civil records such as birth certificates, marriage licenses, and death certificates. Availability of these varies in each country. In the U.S., they are generally available at the state level. Some countries have national-level civil registration. Again, Cyndi's List or an internet search will help you find the links to the state or national vital records offices.

- **Church records:** These records include births, marriages, deaths, confirmation records (useful for estimating a birth date since confirmation usually happened at about age 14), and family registers. Church records often have the most complete record of family events. In times when travel was difficult, civil registration was often deferred or ignored, while births, marriages, and deaths were immediately recorded at the local church. The best way to find these records is usually through the Family History Library (a vast source of genealogical data based in Salt Lake City) and through church archives. It's fun to think that seeing the local church records and finding a new discovery will be part of your visit to an ancestral town. But in many (probably most cases) these records have been consolidated into a central church archive, which is often located in a larger city.

- **Census records:** These records vary in format and content but usually list all members of the family and their ages. They often list where the family came from (at least the country or state), and later U.S. censuses show country of birth, occupation, and other interesting information. Russian censuses also have helped me find out key information about where a family lived in a village and the previous villages where they lived that I hadn't known about.

- **Immigration records:** These types of records may include ships' lists, passport lists, etc. The format and content of each type of record varies, but immigration records are helpful in researching movement from one location to another. These often include all family members and show the place where the family was planning to move.

Be systematic in your approach

As you expand your research efforts, it's best to be systematic in your approach. Start from the information you know and build on that as you work backward in time, discovering new ancestors generation by generation.

Don't make the mistake of generically researching anyone with your family name or researching a famous person with your name, assuming you're somehow related and that your family is from the same places they're from.

For example, I've tracked each birth and marriage of my Schott family ancestors to document their lives in North Dakota, and then prior to that in the German villages in the Black Sea area of Ukraine, and then back to their village in Rheinland-Pfalz, and before that to Hessen. I've resisted the temptation to research Marge Schott, the now deceased, loud-mouthed former owner of the Cincinnati Reds baseball team; Ben Schott, best-selling author; Ernest Schott, my high school librarian; the owners of Schott Music (a multinational music publishing company founded in 1770); or the owners of Schott Glass Corporation (a multinational company focused on glass technology with $2.3 billion in annual sales). All of these are more famous (well, except maybe my high school librarian) than my own Schott family line. But in researching my own line of Schotts back to the 1600s, I have never found a connection with any of these other Schott families. If I'd researched their families, or visited places where those Schotts are from, I would have wasted my time and my travel dollars.

Using Online Resources

Searching online is the best first step to discover the records that are available or the genealogy data that someone else has already found about your family. And it's certainly more convenient (though maybe not as much fun) as a trip to an archive to dig through musty records on your own. There are basically two types of records you'll find online. The first is original sources, and the second is other people's research and family trees.

Original sources

Original sources that are online may include census lists, church records, military records, vital records, etc. In some cases, the actual image of the record will be online. These online images are nirvana to a researcher since the absolute best way to ensure that you are capturing accurate information is by looking at a source yourself.

An extract of a record will generally include all relevant data from the image of the record. For example, an extract of a church marriage

Image of an original EWZ record (Einwanderungzen-tralstelle or Central Immigration Control Department) for Johann Aspenleiter, showing his mother as Helene Kunz, who was the first wife of Valentin Aspenleiter. Record obtained from the U.S. National Archives and Records Administration.

record would include the marriage date, bride and groom's names, and often additional information such as the fathers of the bride and groom or their town of origin. Often extracts are translated into English.

I always recommend verifying the data by looking at the original record to ensure the data has been extracted correctly. If you choose to use an extract as your source record, I recommend adding a note that you haven't verified this yet with the original source. That gives you a record of needed follow-up and allows anyone using your data to understand the limitations of your source information.

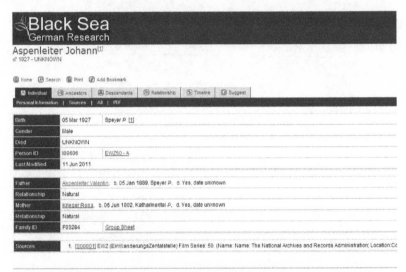

Extract of the EWZ record for Johann Aspenleiter from the Black Sea German Database. This extract is of a different EWZ record than the previous illustration and shows Rosa Krieger, Valentin Aspenleiter's second wife, as the mother of Johann Aspenleiter, rather than Helene Kunz who was listed on the previous EWZ record. This is a great example of why it's important to check original sources and multiple sources.
Courtesy of the Black Sea German Research Community,
www.blackseagr.org.

An index of a record is usually just a finding aid, showing you a key piece of information (such as the person's name) and the page number of the record. To find all the juicy data, you still need to look at the actual record or an extract of the record.

File: 288,163 **EWZ Index for Miscellaneous Films 24 (E. Wise)**

Aspenleiter, Andreas	1 Jul 1923 Sulz	A3343EWZ50-A017 2948	
Aspenleiter, Apollonia	16 Feb 1878 Leonopol	A3343EWZ50-A017 2854	geb. Zent
Aspenleiter, Apollonie	1878 Leonopol	A3343EWZ50-A017 2982	geb. Zent
Aspenleiter, Audenia	2 Oct 1928 Speyer	A3342EWZ50-A018 0030	
Aspenleiter, Barbara	1 Sep 1903 Wolochin	A3343EWZ50-A017 2854	
Aspenleiter, Emilie	7 Feb 1899 Speyer	A3343EWZ50-A017 2890	geb. Schanz
Aspenleiter, Eugenie	23 Jan 1913 Neu Karlsruhe	A3342EWZ50-A017 0012	
Aspenleiter, Filomene	23 Sep 1903 Neu Karlsruh	A3343EWZ50-A017 2914	geb. Schmidt
Aspenleiter, Georg	2 Sep 1896 Speyer	A3343EWZ50-A017 2914	
Aspenleiter, Georg	25 Aug 1923 Neu Karlsruh	A3343EWZ50-A017 2914	
Aspenleiter, Georg	5 Mar 1937 Bratskoje	A3343EWZ50-A017 2854	
Aspenleiter, Jakob	20 Mar 1893 Speyer	A3343EWZ50-A017 2890	
Aspenleiter, Johann	1885 Felsenburg	A3343EWZ50-A017 3002	
Aspenleiter, Johann	5 Mar 1927 Speyer	A3342EWZ50-A018 0030	
Aspenleiter, Johannes	25 Apr 1923 Neu Karlsruhe	A3342EWZ50-A018 0012	
Aspenleiter, Katharine	1864 Speyer	A3342EWZ50-A018 0012	geb. Henrich
Aspenleiter, Katharine	12 Apr 1864 Speyer	A3343EWZ50-A017 2914	geb. Henrich
Aspenleiter, Klementine	11 May 1925 Neu Karlsruh	A3343EWZ50-A017 2914	

*Index listing for Johann Aspenleiter, providing a pointer to the microfilm
with the original image and more information.
Courtesy of the Odessa website, www.odessa3.org.*

Online family trees

The second type of online resource is family trees that others have already researched. These can be an incredibly valuable source of information. These can be an incredibly terrible source of information. Yes, they really are both valuable and terrible.

Online family trees are valuable because it makes sense to share knowledge, and this source can save you from having to retrace research steps completed by another researcher. But there are many pitfalls to be aware of. A couple of these are:

- Not everyone who posts their family trees is a diligent researcher who verifies their sources. Sadly, many people grab information from any source and record it as fact, without ever verifying if it's actually true. I'd hate to visit what I thought was an ancestral town and later find out it is completely unconnected with my family—simply because I trusted a researcher who didn't reliably check their sources.

- Honest mistakes can be perpetuated. For many years, I thought one of my three-times great-grandmothers was Rosina Hensel, first wife of Christian Hinz, simply because I didn't check the dates closely enough to realize my direct ancestor was a child of Christian and his second wife, Wilhelmine Mueller. An honest mistake of mine in working with the church records. When I found it, I fixed it in my family tree. But anyone who looked at my data before I fixed this mistake has the incorrect data . . . and I have no way to tell them that I've corrected my tree.

When you use information from someone else's family tree posted online, always check to see if they have a source listed. But don't stop there—I recommend always looking at that original source to verify the information.

In one online family tree from a researcher I don't know, my grandfather's birthplace is listed as Hoffnungstal, South Russia, and shows the source of that information as his WWI draft registration. But when I looked at his draft registration record for myself, nowhere did it actually show his birthplace.

In this case, I had another source that verified my grandfather's birthplace as Hoffnungstal. But if that researcher had shown my grandfather's birthplace in an incorrect town, and if I accepted the source without checking, I would have the wrong information about my ancestral town. My search would be at a dead end, unable to find previous generations of my ancestors because I'd be looking in the wrong town.

Information in a family tree without a verified source is a good clue but is not reliable data. Never take information from an online source without verifying it for yourself. If you do use information from an online family tree as a clue, be sure to note the researcher and their family tree as one of your sources. This is partly good documentation of your research and partly common courtesy to acknowledge someone else's hard work.

Also, in some cases, a photo or document will be attached to the family tree that you may want to have a copy of. But you should never use a photo or document attached to the family tree (especially if you're planning to publish it in a family history book or website) without getting the permission of the owner. Not only is this common courtesy, but of course it's also important to follow copyright law. (If you have questions on copyright law in the U.S., see www.copyright. gov. If you have questions on copyright law in Canada, see http://laws-lois.justice.gc.ca/eng/acts/C-42/.)

Online genealogy sources

There are more online sources of genealogy information than I can possibly cover in this book, and new ones pop up every day. So I'll just include a sampling of the most important ones.

Family Search (www.familysearch.org)

This is a free site, associated with the Family History Library (FHL), the "mother ship" of all genealogical knowledge. The FHL has been microfilming genealogy records for more than 70 years. As of 2018, it had about 2.4 million rolls of microfilm in its storage site in Utah. There is an enormous effort underway, which includes thousands of volunteers, to index, extract, and digitize this vast collection of genealogical data. Many of the digitized records can be viewed online. In cases where the original archive requested restrictions, the digitized records can be viewed at local branches of the FHL (called Family History Centers) or at designated affiliate libraries.

The FHL's digitized, online data spans the globe. As of 2018, the largest number of online collections are for the U.S. and continental Europe. There are also a large number of collections for the United Kingdom and Ireland, South America, and Canada. Additional collections include: Mexico, Caribbean and Central America, Australia and New Zealand, Asia and Middle East, Africa, and Pacific Islands. (Also keep in mind that the FHL's digitized online data is only the tip of the iceberg. Many of the records I'll describe in the "Moving Beyond Online Resources" section can be found on microfilm in the FHL. Until these are digitized and online, the only way to view them is by visiting the library in Salt Lake City.)

The one caution I have in using this extracted data is that if you find one type of information digitized for a town, don't assume that all the data for that town has been digitized and put online. I found marriage and birth information for my Schott family in the online records for Ober-Gleen, Germany. But the more complete microfilm version of these church records also includes death information that hadn't been digitized yet and provided some key information on my family. If I'd assumed everything for the town was online and didn't search out those death records, I would have missed some important family history.

Family Search also includes a large number of user-submitted genealogy family trees. Again, these are great resources, but don't use the information found there without checking for documented sources and verifying those sources with your own eyes.

Family Search also has some great research guides on their wiki by ethnicity (e.g., German or Irish or Jewish ancestry) or specific topics (e.g., Finding Immigrant Ancestors).

Ancestry (www.ancestry.com)

This is a fee-based subscription service that provides access to an extensive set of records online. In 2017, it claimed to have about 20 billion historical records. These include census and voter lists; birth, marriage, and death records; obituaries; military information; passenger lists; land records; tax lists; church and school directories; maps and gazetteers; and more. Is your head spinning yet?

This can be the mecca of genealogy information, but beware. Ancestry, while a great service, is stronger in their U.S., Canadian, and United Kingdom and Ireland collections than in other parts of the world. If your ancestors have spent the last few hundred years in any of these places, Ancestry will be of great value to you. If, like me, your ancestors were mostly living in other places, you will need to expand your horizons to other sources of information.

In addition to the original documents that are online for subscribers to view, Ancestry also has an extensive set of public member trees that fellow researchers have contributed. These are great sources of information. But as I said previously, use these cautiously. Check for sources and verify any that are noted.

Ancestry has separate websites for the U.S., United Kingdom, Canada, Germany, Italy, Australia, France, and Sweden. Generally, you have the option to either subscribe to the country you're in or, at a higher price, to subscribe to worldwide membership so you can access all available records. As an alternative, many libraries (including Family History Centers and other genealogy organization libraries) have a worldwide subscription that you can access on the library's computers.

Cyndi's List (www.cyndislist.com)

Cyndi's List, a volunteer effort by Cyndi Ingle, is the ultimate set of links one can ever hope to find for genealogy. While Cyndi's List doesn't have actual records available, it does provide links to anything and everything genealogical. Looking for how to get started? Looking for genealogy blogs? Looking for vital records for your Cajun ancestors? Trying to figure out an unusual calendar entry in a record? Looking for information on royalty or genealogy software or creating a family history book or hiring a professional researcher? Cyndi's List has got you covered.

Find a Grave (www.findagrave.com)

Find a Grave is a volunteer-based site that catalogs gravestones and cemeteries. With a database of 162 million grave records in more than 400,000 cemeteries in more than 200 countries (as of 2017), it is an incredible source to help find your ancestors' last resting place and any information from their headstones. Some entries include photos of the headstones.

USGenWeb (usgenweb.org) and RootsWeb (www.rootsweb.ancestry.com)

USGenWeb and RootsWeb are websites of free genealogical information for the U.S., maintained by volunteers. Since the records included are at the discretion (or whim) of the volunteers, the types of records you'll find might seem a bit random. But these are still great places to find vital records, cemetery transcriptions, county histories, maps, etc., from people who really know their local areas. The websites also include online forums, where you can post questions and interact with other researchers. These forums are searchable, and the questions and answers are archived, which allows you to connect with researchers who may have posted a question months previously. I solved one family mystery because another researcher, who had the parts of the genealogical puzzle I lacked, found my inquiry on a forum a year after I posted it.

USGenWeb is organized primarily at the state level, while RootsWeb is more focused on county-specific records. RootsWeb, although recently taken over by Ancestry, remains free at the time I'm writing this.

WorldGen Web (www.worldgenweb.org)

WorldGenWeb is also run by volunteers and includes free genealogical information or links to research resources for numerous countries around the world. The site also includes good historical background that may help you better understand what records to look for.

Ellis Island (www.ellisisland.org), Castle Garden (www.castlegarden.org), German Roots (www.germanroots.com/passengers.html) and Steve Morse's site (www.stevemorse.org)

When you think of an immigrating ancestor, you usually think of Ellis Island. And why not? About 40 percent of Americans have ancestors who arrived through Ellis Island. So the Ellis Island database of more than 20 million arrival records between 1892 and 1924 can be a juicy find for your research. These records, especially the later ones that have more information, can often be helpful in identifying your ancestor's place of origin.

Of course, not everyone's ancestors came through Ellis Island, even if they arrived during the height of the immigration center's activity. When I couldn't find several Schott and Siewert ancestors at El-lis Island, I was very disappointed. And then I did the research I should have done in the first place and went back to find their Declarations of Intent paperwork, which was required between 1790 and 1952 for anyone who wanted to apply for U.S. citizenship. These showed they'd arrived through Baltimore and Canada rather than through Ellis Island.

Also, the Ellis Island indexes were created by volunteers who might have struggled with deciphering the handwriting or with unusu-al foreign family names. If you don't immediately find your ancestor in the index but know they arrived through New York, it's worth doing a little additional digging because they simply may have been indexed incorrectly.

If your ancestors arrived prior to 1892, they would have entered New York through Castle Garden, which was an earlier immigrant processing center. The Castle Garden site has records from 1820 to 1913, although the majority of records are from prior to 1892.

A useful tool in searching these (and other) sites is on Steve Morse's site, which provides finding aids for the Ellis Island and Castle Garden sites, a selection of other passenger lists, and a variety of other useful records. Another helpful site for finding resources for passenger lists is Joe Beine's www.germanroots.org/passengers.html site (not just for those with German ancestry).

Genealogybank (www.genealogybank.com)

Genealogybank is a fee-based, but interesting, site with a great col-lection of U.S. newspapers and obituaries online, as well as a number of other historical documents. The collection of newspapers spans 1690-2010 and even includes some of the small-town Dakota news-papers where my family lived (the type of resource that is sometimes hard to find online). The obituaries are priceless to genealogists, and you can also find a number of interesting articles about your ancestors. (I wonder if it was really my grandfather Peter Schott who suffered from a bout of food poisoning in 1921?)

Honorable mention sites

Websites come and go, and each of you will have a very specific research path depending on your ethnic heritage, so it's impossible to include an exhaustive list of genealogy websites. Cyndi's List is most helpful for digging around to find all the sites most useful for your specific search. But there are a few additional sites worth mentioning:

- **Allen County Public Library** (www.genealogycenter.org): One of the largest genealogy collections available.
- **New England Historic Genealogical Society** (library.ne-hgs.org/): Most useful if you have roots in colonial America, but they have a number of other useful records too.
- **The Federation of Genealogical Societies** (www.fgs.org): To help find a genealogy organization near you or specific to your ethnic heritage.
- **Chronicling America** (chroniclingamerica.loc.gov/search/titles/): A site from the Library of Congress that helps identify historic newspapers from your ancestors' local areas. Its holdings information may not be totally up-to-date though, since it was missing information about at least one Dakotas-based German-language paper that I've used for my research.
- **OnlineNewspapers.com** (www.onlinenewspapers.com): A site to help you find out if a newspaper useful to your research is available online.
- **Facebook** (www.facebook.com): Love it or hate it, Facebook has become a powerful tool for genealogy, enabling you to network with others through numerous groups available for every aspect of genealogy you can think of, from DNA to Vikings to everything in between.
- **Black Sea German Research Community** (www.blackseagr.org): If you share my heritage of ethnic Germans who lived in the Black Sea area of Imperial Russia, this website has a growing database of family trees and lots of resources available for

researching this ethnic group. Full disclosure—it was started and is run by myself and some of my best genealogy buddies.

Moving Beyond Online Resources

We'd all like to find our ancestors with a couple clicks of a mouse on a laptop. And with an increasing number of genealogy records online, it seems like we should all be able to find our ancestors while sitting comfortably in our own living rooms.

But I have yet to meet a researcher who has been able to find their family roots relying only on online sources. At some point in your search, you'll need to dig into records in archives, libraries, or county courthouses to find your ancestors. Here's an overview of some of the key resources you'll need to be familiar with to research your family.

Birth records

There are a number of different types of documents that can be included in the category of birth records, including:

- Church birth records, usually available from the FHL or from a church archive, sometimes from the actual church.
- Civil birth records, available from state or county vital records offices (in the U.S.) or national civil records agencies.
- Birth certificates and baptismal certificates, which you may find in a family member's attic or closet. A stepcousin of mine found my mother's and grandmother's beautifully decorated baptismal certificates in my stepaunt's attic and rescued them from oblivion (aka my stepaunt's garbage).

Birth records document the date and location of your ancestors' births. They also usually show the parents' names (or at least the father's name), which helps you find the previous generation. Some birth records also show the child's godparents, which can be useful in unraveling family relationships since the godparents were usually relatives. In at least one case I've seen, the godparents from out of town provided a clue to the mother's maiden name and her birthplace.

Marriage records

These include church marriage records, civil marriage records, and marriage certificates. At minimum, a marriage record will include the bride and groom's names and the date and location of the marriage. But marriage records often include the couple's parents' names (or at least the fathers' names), helping you find that previous generation. They may list the town or profession of the groom (as weddings often took place in the bride's hometown). They may give the age of the bride and groom (useful for estimating their birth years) or some information about previous marriages (if the bride/groom is a widow or widower). The marriage record of my five-times great-grandfather Michael Schott in Osthofen led me back a generation to his father, also Michael Schott, from Ober-Gleen, Germany.

Death records

These include church death records, civil death records, and death certificates, as well as obituaries and informal death notices in newspapers. Death records usually include the name of the deceased and date and place of death. They sometimes include the cause of death and the birthplace of the deceased. This is a great clue for research, but remember that the person (usually the spouse or child of the deceased) giving the information may not know the correct location. The death record may also include the birth date of the deceased, or at least their age at death, to help you guesstimate the birth date. Obituaries and other death notices in newspapers often will list surviving family members and include additional biographical information that can help you learn more about the life of the deceased.

Church family registers

Some churches kept registers that list family groups—first the mother and father, then children in birth order. These are useful as it can be difficult to be sure you've found all the children or know which ones are associated with which parents if multiple marriages are involved. Family registers list birth, death, marriage, and confirmation dates and locations for each person. These can be really useful if the family moved from another village as the family register will generally show where the parents were born or married. These records would usually be available in church archives or through the FHL.

Census records

If birth/marriage/death records aren't available for your family, census records can be a valuable source of information because they list all family members, their ages, and sometimes the locations where the family lived previously. U.S. census records are available online (for privacy reasons, those less than 70 years old are not available), but census records for other countries may not be. To find census records, check civil archives for the country you are interested in, genealogy societies for the area you are searching, or Cyndi's List to find links to these.

Town history books

In the U.S. and Canada, many towns created history books for special town anniversary celebrations. These books often have family histories and include valuable information about family members, dates, and locations as well as family biographies. Towns in Germany often have Ortssippenbücher (town lineage books), which give history about the town and may include very detailed family genealogical data. Wherever your ancestral town is located, it's worth trying to locate any books from that town that include specific family information. The FHL has many of these in their collection, or contact a library or town hall in your ancestral town to see if your town has a book with this sort of information.

The church in Ober-Gleen, Germany

In Their Footsteps

Off the Tourist Track
(Original blog post: April 27, 2010)

Castles, cathedrals, Oktoberfest, cruising the Rhine River—these are the things most people go to Germany to experience. But my itinerary was one you wouldn't find in a tour book: the local museum in a small town, the village church and cemetery, and the small Kunst im Kuhstall (Art in the Cowstall) art gallery. I was visiting Ober-Gleen, the home of my Schott ancestors in the 1600s.

Although Ober-Gleen and Kirtorf (the neighboring town that is now the central administration for seven villages, including Ober-Gleen) lie on the Deutsch Märchenstraße (German Fairy Tale Road) in the Vogelsberg region (a popular area for outdoor activities), they won't be found in any guide book. Which is a shame, because they are charming examples of small-town Germany.

My host for the day was the owner of the art gallery, Herr Bloemers, a retiree from the hotel industry after managing five-star hotels in numerous countries throughout his career (which made his English far better than my German). Although the gallery was quiet the day I was there, its popularity is evident since the exhibit space is already booked a year in advance and opening parties usually include guests from Frankfurt (about an hour's drive away).

I'll admit, I expected the Kirtorf museum would be a typical local museum—poorly lit with a dusty collection of 19th century furniture and other items from people's attics. Instead, behind its historic *fachwerk* exterior, it was a completely renovated, bright space with well-explained displays and innovative audio-visuals.

One exhibit area explained the Schmeerofen, a process that produced wagon wheel lubricant from sticky tree pitch (who knew such a thing was possible?), which was important to the area's economy for many decades. Only a small number of places throughout Germany had the right type of trees to use for this process.

Another exhibit was devoted to Friedrich Ludwig Weidig, a pastor for a time in Ober-Gleen, who was active in a Germany-wide movement in the 1830s that had the audacity to suggest that all the German principalities should become one nation (which finally occurred in 1871). He was arrested for his "radical" political beliefs and finally committed suicide while in prison.

Looking for traces of my ancestors

But what about my own family history? Well, when I went to the bank to exchange money, it was clear the Schott name no longer held any weight here. The first bank wouldn't exchange my dollars at all, saying something about my needing an account there. The tellers at the second bank laughingly suggested to Herr Bloemers that the problem might have been caution in taking dollars from a random (possibly suspicious) American showing up at their counter.

Of course, they also laughed when I asked for euros. Though I spoke in German, I used the American pronunciation for euros, which sounds like the German pronunciation for gyros, the Greek fast food. Hmm, maybe the first bank thought I was ordering lunch rather than exchanging currency?

Although I know my Schott ancestors lived in Ober-Gleen in the 1600s and early 1700s, there's little trace of them today. The cemetery of that time was next to the church and is now a parking lot. The current church wasn't built until 1735, when my ancestor Michael Schott had already left the village. But the baptismal font dates back to the 1500s, so it was probably used to baptize some of my Schott ancestors.

There are no Schott family members in the village today, although other names associated with my family (Mess, Fröhlich, Schleich, Jacobi, Stumpf) still exist there. I probably have some distant cousins in Ober-Gleen, descendents of Michael's sisters. But I don't have enough information to make the connection and neither do they. As Herr Bloemers explained to me, "They know their families have always lived here. Family history is just not so interesting to them."

A day in Ober-Gleen

My day in Ober-Gleen was not a usual tourist day of jostling with crowds to take photos of big-name sights.

But learning about the local history and seeing the museum . . . having the typical German afternoon coffee and cake in the April sunshine as classical music drifted from the gallery . . . eating dinner in the local Gastätte where the mayor greeted each person while he shared an after-work beer with those at the bar . . . seeing the memorial to the Jewish families who had lived here until WWII . . . watching the Gleenbach brook tumble along the edge of the village as a bicyclist coasted over one of its bridges . . . spending the night in the Kirtorf hotel with its historic restaurant but thoroughly modern rooms (and eating some of the best spätzle I've tasted) . . . seeing the local fachwerk houses in their natural habitat (far more interesting than visiting the nearby open-air museum, even one as well-done as Hessen Park) . . . all these things created a special visit for me to this little village off the tourist track.

Chapter 3

Strategies for Successful Research

The baptismal font in Ober-Gleen, Germany where my five-times great-grandfather Michael Schott was baptized.

Key Tips for Your Research

Now that you have an understanding of the types of records available for your research, it's time to think about some strategies for approaching your research and tips for success.

Network, network, network!

Hanging out with other genealogists is one of the most effective ways to find those hard-to-find records or little-known bits of history that could be the key to unlocking a family mystery. Join your local genealogy society. Join genealogy groups that relate to your specific family roots. (I'm a member of several groups that specialize in researching ethnic Germans who lived in Eastern Europe.) Join groups and follow relevant pages on Facebook, or search out genealogy experts on Twitter. These are the people who are most likely to know how to find records that might not be in one of the big online databases.

These groups and contacts will be useful not only in doing your research but may also be helpful in planning your trip to visit your ancestral town. They can help you find tour planners with specialized knowledge for your area or identify contacts at archives you want to visit. Being a member of such a group may even help you find like-minded friends to travel with, which is what happened for me!

Keep an open mind

Spellings change. Don't assume that the way you spell a name now (both family names and locations) is the only way it has ever been spelled. And don't assume that your names were written correctly by every census taker or every church scribe. I've seen my Dickhoff name spelled Dikhoff, Dikhof, Dickhof, Dikow, and Дикоф (and I'm still wondering about any connection with Dikopf and Dickhaut). My friend Rich has found 14 different spelling variations of his name, Aspenleiter.

Other names have even more variation. I recently discovered that the original spelling of one family name from the Alsace region, "Schack," appears to have started out as the French name, "Jacques," which actually sounds similar though I would never have thought of that variation.

Having an open mind about spelling was also instrumental in my finding the town where my Schott family originated in Germany. A marriage record for Michael Schott said he came from Oberklein, Hessen. Through a series of serendipitous pointers from fellow genealogists, I followed a trail from Oberklein to Oberkleen to Ober-Gleen, Hessen, and found my guy in the church records there. Be creative.

Keep an open mind, too, on things that "everyone" knows. Assumptions like "Back in those days, Catholics never married Lutherans" or "Christians never married Jews" or "Everyone in that village came from a certain location" or "The first son is always named after his paternal grandfather" can lead you in the wrong direction or cause errors in the data you gather. Every family has exceptions. You may overlook some good clues or get your family information wrong by assuming that what "everyone knows" is true for your family.

Name variations

In addition to spelling variations, keep in mind that names can vary in other ways. Know the ethnic variations for the name you're searching for. John, Johann, Hans, Yiannis, Janos, Ivan, and Giovanni are all variations of the same name. My grandfather was born Johann Peter, but every source in the U.S. shows him as John Peter. Same guy, different country, different ethnic variation of the name.

The website BehindtheName.com is useful for figuring out the variations for which you should keep your eyes open.

For surnames, some of the variations that commonly occurred are:
- Literal translations (the German surname Weber is changed to Weaver, or the French name LeBlanc is changed to White).
- Shortening names (the name Weisspfennig is changed to Weiss). Who knows, if your ancestor was really creative, he may have lengthened his name in some unpredictable way too.
- Try substituting like-sounding letters (the name Bitz could be spelled Pitz, or the name Klein could become Glein).

Be cautious about what you "know" to be true

Sometimes even what you personally absolutely believe to be true isn't. I was completely certain that I knew all about my Uncle Danny. We visited his family every summer. I hung out with my cousins. My mom always talked about her brother. So of course, I never thought to verify any information about him with vital records or church records.

It took another researcher's database for me to find out that his legal name was Wilbert Theodore. At first, I thought that researcher had bad data, until I asked my mom about this. She said, "Oh yes, he hated his real name and wouldn't use it. He just took his nickname from his dad's name. Didn't I ever tell you that?" Uh, no.

Remember what I said about verifying every piece of information against original records? I should have taken my own advice.

Search both backwards and sideways in time

Even if your main interest in genealogy is searching backwards in time to find your many-times great-grandparents and the towns where they lived, it also pays to search sideways in time by connecting with distant cousins or researching your direct ancestor's siblings or cousins.

Another branch of the family might have a photo or other documentation that you don't have. In my case, connecting with a third cousin in Montana led me to a letter written two generations previously by her direct ancestor about our mutual great-great-grandparents and their parents. For many years, this letter was the only hard evidence I had of my three-times great-grandparents since the church records from the early years of Germans living in the Black Sea region had been destroyed.

Sometimes researching the siblings of your ancestor can help you locate the family. If your direct ancestors were evasive in recording what town they were born in or what ship they traveled on, you can sometimes track down the family by researching a sibling who was more forthcoming with information. For example, my Siewert three-times great-grandfather consistently showed his birthplace only as Poland or Prussia, while his younger brother was a little more detail-oriented and recorded his birthplace as Plock, Poland. Although I can't just assume that August (my direct ancestor) was born in the same place as younger brother Karl, this at least gives me a starting place within all of Poland to look for records.

And sometimes connecting with distant cousins is just fun. Through genealogy, I got to know my third cousin once removed, Ute, who lives in Germany. We found out we have lots of things in common and became friends in addition to being distant cousins. I've stayed at her place, and we've roamed around Germany. We've road tripped together through the Dakotas (and Iowa and Minnesota) meeting up with cousins. Just recently, I managed to get to Germany for her dad's 80th birthday celebration. Who knew I'd form new international friendships through my search?

Focus on one ancestral line at a time

It's tempting to dive in and research all your grandparents or great-grandparents at once, trying to find out as much as you can about all of them. But I've found it is often better to really concentrate on one line at a time, following the clues and figuring out where to look next.

Genealogy can sometimes be a bit of an art, requiring some creativity to solve the intricate puzzle of your roaming ancestors. I've often found myself noodling on some missing data, "Hmm, if one clue suggests they were in this town in 1816, but no record actually shows them there until 1829, where could they have been in the meantime?" and suddenly a new possibility pops in my head to research.

If you're merely trying to accumulate data about all your family lines, your mind goes on overload. It can be difficult to remember what stage your research is at for each family line, which may keep you from having the mental bandwidth to let your creative problem-solving juices flow.

Focusing on one ancestral line at a time also helps keep you organized so you can file all the records you discover (whether actual paper or digital copies) by family line. Sometimes the joy of the discovery overcomes my inner organizer and chaos reigns in my genealogy paperwork. Don't let it happen to you.

Know the history of the area you're researching

Knowing the history of the area where your family lived is helpful in better understanding your ancestors' lives and giving you at least a little insight into their hopes and dreams and fears, even if you don't (as I don't) have any family diaries or personal papers. This can help you understand their lives and decisions better, such as why they chose to migrate or practice their particular trade. But just as important, a good understanding of the history of the area you're researching can provide valuable clues to your genealogy. Understanding the governments in power or the political situation will help you find out what records are available and where they might be. (Alas, I wish everything was conveniently located in Ancestry or the FHL, but many, many records exist outside those vast libraries and databases.)

Understanding the history of specific time periods may also help you judge the accuracy of any data you find. In some cases, stressful situations can lead to inaccurate records—either because your ancestors simply couldn't remember important information in the middle of a war (or other crisis) or needed to hide something (children's ages, the family's religion) to protect the family.

Diving into the history of the region you're researching can also help you find your family. When researching my Klein family, Lutherans who had lived in Hungary, I knew my ancestor Matthias was born in 1769 in a town called Jenk. I assumed that Jenk had to be in Germany because Matthias lived in an area of Hungary that had been settled by German Protestants in the 1780s, when he would already have been a teenager. Although there had been earlier waves of German immigration to Hungary, all my sources said that only German Catholics were allowed in the earlier groups of immigrants. I assumed he must have been born in Germany and arrived in Hungary with the later wave of Protestant immigrants.

I searched high and low throughout Germany for a town with a similar name with no luck.

Fortunately, I found a history book that didn't just tell the official story but described what actually happened. Officially, the Austrian-Hungarian government only allowed Catholics in the groups that came between 1718 and 1772. In reality, many Protestants were also included among those immigrants. In some cases, they had to convert to Catholicism, and in others, they settled on the estates of religiously tolerant landowners.

Once I expanded my search for Jenk to include Hungary, I found it relatively easily as Gyönk. And I discovered that my Klein family had arrived in Hungary two generations earlier than I'd expected—probably among the first to make the journey.

I would never have located those two generations without deepening my knowledge of the history of the migration of Germans to Hungary.

Be creative

Be willing to go beyond traditional genealogical sources. In researching her French-Canadian family, my friend Jackie discovered that one of her relatives had been the executive assistant to Edsel Ford (son of Henry Ford and president of the Ford Motor Company in the 1920s through early '40s). This relative had even been named the executor of Ford's estate. By writing the Ford Company, my friend obtained extensive historical information about her ancestor from the company's 50th anniversary publication.

A car company is hardly a traditional source of genealogical information, but being creative paid off for my friend.

Finding Those Hard-to-Find Ancestral Towns

So far, we've focused on the strategies and resources that every genealogist uses to research their family roots. But, of course, your special interest is in finding the locations your ancestors came from so you can walk in their footsteps. For those of us in North America, "jumping the pond" to figure out where our families lived previously can be the most difficult part of our search. Official documents like censuses and citizenship papers allowed our ancestors to be vague about the details of their birthplaces—adequate for the official purposes of the time, but very frustrating for us as researchers. Here are a few ideas to find the birthplaces of your elusive ancestors.

Obituaries and death notices

Death can be very helpful in finding the specific town and location names for your ancestors. Obituaries, informal death notices in newspapers, and even gravestones can be a great source of information. Even if great-grandpa didn't feel the need to tell the census taker anything more than "England" or "Ohio," he probably told his children or grandchildren stories about where he came from, and they are the ones who filled out the death certificate or wrote the obituary.

Of course, that can also lead to misunderstandings. My mother grew up in the town of Lehr and always talked about it as her hometown. It wasn't until I started doing research that I realized she'd actually been born in the neighboring town of Kulm. I was able to make sure my mother's obituary was correct, but I only knew the right information because of my genealogy research. If I'd written it based on what she'd told me all my life, I would have listed the wrong town.

Family papers

Not everyone is lucky enough to inherit an attic full, or even a handful, of treasured family documents. But if you're one of the lucky ones, go through these with a fine-tooth comb to see what clues you can find. Family letters, wills, wedding announcements, even photos (which may have location clues written on the back or names of neighbors that might provide clues) may help you narrow down your search for your family's place of origin.

My friend Jackie's French-Canadian great-grandfather deserted his wife, leaving behind neither support for his young children nor clues to his family heritage. But among her grandmother's papers, Jackie discovered a 1923 letter from a nun in Wisconsin who happened to be her grandmother's cousin. The letter included information about the brother of Jackie's great-grandfather, who was the nun's father. This gave Jackie a new branch of the family to research, which might provide some clues to finding her elusive ancestor's family origins and place of birth.

Local sources

Does the town where your family lived have a historical society or publish any books about the town's history? Was your ancestor a business person or leader in town government who might have had biographical information included in the local newspaper? In many towns, even events like having an out-of-town visitor might have been newsworthy enough to get your ancestor mentioned.

Was your ancestor a leader in a local church that might have archive materials, such as church meeting minutes or publications? If you don't know which church your ancestor went to, use the census and city directories to locate churches near their home. Contact the churches to see what records or publications might be available to verify whether your ancestors attended there.

Network with other researchers familiar with the region you're researching as they might be aware of hard-to-locate resources. In the Dakotas, where my family comes from, there were a couple of German-language newspapers (the *Dakota Freie Presse* and the *Staats-Anzeiger*) that published letters submitted by their readers. People from villages in Bessarabia, Ukraine, would commonly write to their own family in the Dakotas and include messages like, "Please let my old friend Peter Schott know that his mother passed away in November." When these letters were published in the local German-language newspapers, all people who were originally from that village got to hear a little bit about home. A source like this can also help you locate your family's origin.

Fellow genealogists, local libraries, and historical societies may all help you find sources unique to your area. They also can help you identify which resources are available online and which you need to access physical or microfilm copies at a library or archive.

Sibling rivalry

If your direct ancestors were too tight-lipped to give away their birthplace, try researching their siblings. And cousins. And aunts and uncles—any family member you can track down. One of them must have mentioned their town to someone, so it will show up in their obituary or another record, providing you with a clue to follow up on your own ancestor. This is a good time to track down those distant cousins and see what their branch of the family knows that you can't find.

Neighbors forever

Well, maybe not forever. But it is true that people often traveled to the same place their neighbors did. Fellow Black Sea German researchers have told me that their family's neighbors in the Dakotas in the 1900s were the same families they lived near and intermarried with in the Black Sea region in the 1800s, which were the same families they lived near and intermarried with in Poland in the late 1700s, which were the same families they lived near and intermarried with in Germany in the early 1700s.

So if you strike out in researching family members, start looking at their neighbors to see if you can identify where they came from. Families who were close to yours may show up near them in the census records, or you may see significant numbers of intermarriages between your family and theirs. Try the same sources I suggested above (obituaries and local sources) to try to identify these neighbors' hometowns.

In addition, this is a really good way to use online family trees— connecting with researchers with similar interests. If you can find these neighbors' names in an online family tree database (Ancestry, Family Search, or any that are specific to your own area of research), these are generally set up so you can easily contact the researcher interested in that family. That researcher may have discovered some information you haven't about where their family came from.

But be cautious not to assume too much. Just because your family seemed close to another family, you can't assume without further documentation that's where your family is from too. It's simply one more tool that provides a clue in your search.

Ships' passenger lists

Finding the ship's passenger list for your immigrant ancestor may open an important door to finding out where your ancestor came from and how they journeyed to North America.

During the colonial period and through 1820, passenger records are scarce. Some are available through Ancestry. In addition, the German Roots website (www.germanroots.com/1820.html) has a good bibliography of pre-1820 passenger list resources (not just for those of German heritage).

After 1820, an act of Congress resulted in passenger lists being more consistently recorded. However, until 1906, passenger lists for people entering the U.S. still allowed very vague descriptions of a passenger's place of origin. In 1906, passenger manifests were required to add the name and address of the closest living relative in their country of origin. If you're lucky enough to have ancestors arriving in this later time period, passenger lists might give you the clue you need.

Naturalization records

If your ancestor became a citizen between 1790 and 1952, they had to follow a two-step process: first to declare their intent to become a citizen and then, two to five years later, to actually petition for citizenship. Until 1922, a woman's citizenship status was based on her husband's (she became a citizen when her husband did; and if she married a non-citizen, she lost her citizenship). Until 1940, children's citizenship was based on their father's status.

Although the Declaration of Intent and Petition for Naturalization forms left our ancestors the option to be vague about their origins ("Ireland" doesn't narrow down your search much; it's a big island), some people were more forthcoming, and you might find some useful information from naturalization records to track back to where your ancestor came from.

Emigration indexes

You generally know where your ancestors ended up, but if they weren't cooperative enough to record where they came from before that, an emigration index might help. (Emigration is where your ancestor came from. Immigration is where your ancestor went to. My great-grandfather Daniel Netz emigrated from Ukraine. He immigrated to North Dakota.)

In places where residents had to get permission to leave, such as Württemberg, Germany, in the 1800s, there are often civic records of those who emigrated. If you can narrow down the possible locations they might have come from, you can search a bit more efficiently. Knowing that my ancestors came from Germany enables me to skip Australian or Irish emigration indexes. But if I can figure out that they came from the state of Württemberg or Rheinland-Pfalz, that narrows down my search even further to a more concentrated set of indexes.

Search Cyndi's List or Ancestry for online emigration lists. In addition, some are available primarily in book format—check the FHL or civil archives of the locality for which you are searching.

Military records

Enlistment records can give you a pointer to your ancestor's place of birth, even if it is located overseas. The most frequently searched records are those associated with a specific war or military conflict (WWI, WWII, etc.). In addition, the "U.S. Army Register of Enlistments 1798-1914" and the "U.S. Marine Corps Muster Rolls 1798-1940" may have records, and places of birth, for ancestors who served in the military but didn't enlist at the time of a specific conflict. These records are available through the National Archives (www.archives.gov/research/military/) and through Ancestry (www.ancestry.com).

U.S. Citizenship and Immigration Services (USCIS)

Even if your immigrant ancestor never became a citizen, there may be some records with USCIS (www.uscis.gov/historyandgenealogy), such as alien registration forms, that may help you pinpoint where they came from.

Places with multiple names

I've had some special challenges finding the locations of my ancestral towns because my ancestors were ethnic Germans living in what is now Ukraine or Moldova. They had German names for the towns, which carry down today in any stories told by my grandparents or great-grandparents, but these names are not to be found on any current-day map.

If you have a similar challenge searching for your ancestors, be sure to seek out genealogy groups that specialize in your ethnic origins. By using sources from "Germans from Russia" groups, I've been able to find maps and locations of my villages by finding the German names I know cross-referenced with the current-day Ukrainian or Moldovan names.

Check for reference books that may have this sort of cross-index of names. Two I discovered for German research are the *Amtliches Gemeinde- und Ortsnamenverzeichnis der Deutschen Ostgebiete unter fremder Verwaltung* and *Deutsch-fremdsprachiges Ortsnamenverzeichnis*, which show a cross-reference of German village names with the name in the local language.

Another challenge is that your ancestor might have come from a small town. Assuming no one would ever have heard of it, they filled out their paperwork with the name of a larger, more well-known town; just as today, someone who comes from the small town of Puyallup may tell people they're from Seattle, even though it's 40 miles away, because Seattle is more well-known.

And of course, you need to be aware of translations of the place names you're researching. Bavaria and Latvia are Bayern and Lettland in German. Some translations are not at all obvious. For example, the Baltic Sea is Ostsee (literally, East Lake) in German.

Borders change

Yet another challenge in discovering your ancestral town is that the tides of history and national borders ebb and flow, making it difficult to identify the town based on your ancestors' descriptions and to figure out where to find records. My ancestors lived in an area that belonged to the Turks before they moved there, then became part of Russia, then part of Romania, then Russia again, and is currently partly in Ukraine and partly in Moldova's breakaway republic of Transdniester. Other ancestors lived in an area that alternated at a dizzying speed between being owned by Poland, Prussia, and Russia. When my ancestors noted their place of birth as Prussia, it doesn't help me much to narrow in on their location.

For a really vivid example of how borders changed in Europe from the 1200s to recent times, this video is excellent: https://www.youtube.com/watch?v=M90C7FA4FYU.

How does it sound?

In addition to looking at the name of an ancestral town in writing, think about how it sounds. Some letters can sound alike and could be written in different ways, making it difficult to find the village on a map. Some letters that I've had breakthroughs with were g and k, d and t, and b and p.

Wesley is standing between my grandparents

In Their Footsteps

The Elusive Wesley
(Original blog post: April 7, 2018)

I know he existed. But where did he go?

One of our family mysteries is Wesley, an orphan boy that lived with my Schott grandparents sometime in the early 1900s. The family lore is that my Grandpa Peter "went to the train station" to pick him up, that he was a bit wild, and that he died when he fell off a horse, hitting his head on a rock because his feet were stuck in the stirrups. The story about him being "wild" is either connected to the fall, or to the story that he used to load my young aunt and uncles into a wagon and then have a horse pull them around the farmyard.

What I find so mysterious is that Wesley is not listed in the North Dakota state death index nor in the records of the Kulm Congregational Church, the Schott family's church. Why wouldn't his death be recorded in one of these places?

What I know

I have a photo, so I know he lived with my grandparents' family in 1914. In that photo, I'm guessing he's between 10 and 13 years old (maybe a bit older if he's not standing on something to make him taller).

He's on the 1915 North Dakota state census as "Wesle Schott." That indicates to me that, whether they adopted him officially or not, they considered him a member of the family. But he's gone by the next U.S. census, recorded in January 1920.

My wild speculations

I know that I need to focus my search based on what I know, at least until I prove that it's wrong. But I can't help speculating.

What if he didn't really die (since I can't find his death record), but instead ran off and became a WWI doughboy?

Could he have come from the Orphan Train (based on the reference to my grandfather picking him up at the train station)? But when I contacted the Orphan Train Society, they could find nothing on him. Of course, I didn't have much information to work with, not even his real last name.

Could he have been Catholic? Many of the Orphan Train riders were Irish Catholics from New York. In the early 20th century, it might not have been considered proper to record the death of a Catholic boy in the records of a Protestant church.

Where I'm looking

But going back to what I've been told—that he died while living with my grandparents—I devised a plan to search the 1915 through 1920 issues of the local paper, the *Kulm Messenger*, while I was in Kulm for Easter this year. Even if his death didn't get recorded officially, I'm sure such a tragic accident would have made it into the paper.

Unfortunately, timing issues and snowy roads cut into my research time, and I was only able to search one out of the five years I needed to look at. (Bad microfilm didn't help my cause . . . being hard to read made it difficult to scan quickly and slowed me down.)

No luck so far, and the mystery continues to be unsolved. A dark chocolate mocha soothed my disappointment as I made plans to return.

Chapter 4

Searching Your Roots with DNA

Embracing my German ethnicity by "dressing up"
as a typical German woman of the 1800s.

So What About DNA?

DNA seems like a fun and easy way to cut through all the research time and immediately find out your roots, doesn't it? A little spit in a tube or a cheek swab, and voilà! You immediately know how Irish or Chinese or Norwegian or Kenyan you are, and you can be off on a visit to your ancestral homeland.

The consumer genetic testing business is growing at an astounding rate. The number of people who have had their DNA analyzed doubled in 2017 and totaled an estimated 12 million at the beginning of 2018 (*MIT Technology Review*, 12 February 2018). It's become a popular stocking stuffer gift, and a subject of casual conversation at the office: "Oh yes, my husband found out he's part Middle Eastern. How cool is that?"

Finding out your ethnic roots through a DNA test is lots of fun. But it can also be confusing and concerning when the results don't match what you've always known about your heritage. Panic can set in—what if I'm not really who I think I am? What if my parents aren't really my parents?

You may think, "DNA is a scientific certainty. DNA doesn't lie." While that's true, the analysis of DNA to determine ethnicity is much more art than science, based on a number of estimates.

Bottom line—hold off before booking your trip to an ancestral land based on only your DNA ethnicity results. But DNA testing can be useful—we'll talk about that too.

Exploring DNA ethnicity results

When I did my first DNA test and it showed a huge percentage of Eastern European, I first wondered if an NPE (not parent expected or non-paternity event) had occurred in my ancestral line—a situation where the father I've documented through records was not the actual biological father. My ancestors lived in Eastern Europe, but they were ethnic Germans according to every record I've found. I wondered if one of my ancestresses had an encounter with one of the locals outside her German village in Ukraine or Poland.

But as I learned more about ethnicity tests, I realized that the ethnicity test alone was not enough to worry about such a gap in my paper documentation. The testing companies are doing their best to identify your origin from about 500 years ago when, theoretically, our ancestors didn't move around much. But they don't have 500-year-old DNA to use for comparison. So they rely on reference populations of individuals today who seem to have deep roots in specific locations. Each testing company defines their geographic areas differently, so people from border areas of their expected region may show up differently when testing with different companies. And our ancestors actually did move around, even 500 years ago, more than you might expect.

I've tested or uploaded my DNA to four of the DNA testing

companies offering genealogy testing services, as well as the National Geographic Geno DNA test (more useful for deep origin information than for genealogy research) and GEDmatch (an online tool for analyzing DNA). All six of their ethnicity tests come back with wildly different results—from each other and from my documented heritage. (For more on this, see my blog post at the end of this chapter.)

Every ancestor I've found (and I have all of my lines into the 1700s, some into the 1500s) are documented as ethnic Germans, with the one possible exception of an ancestor that I suspect (but haven't proven) is a French Huguenot. Yet until recently, only one of my DNA tests showed a sizeable chunk of German heritage for me. Many do show large percentages for me as "General European" or "Northern and Western Europe." Of course, this is all true, as Germany lies in this region. It's just not very targeted or helpful.

Various results show my heritage as Baltic, Balkan, Scandinavian, or Mediterranean. And 4.2 percent West Asian? I suppose that could be attributed to some leftover DNA from Genghis Khan and his Mongol hordes overrunning Europe (which is actually sort of an intriguing heritage to be able to claim). But it's hard to reconcile with any of my documented ancestry.

I'm having a lot of fun figuring this all out and trying to sort out the differences. For example, if the Baltic heritage shows up on my Siewert line, which is most likely from northeastern Germany near the Baltic Sea, then the apparently contradictory results actually make sense.

But I'm finding that rather than focus on ethnicity estimates, DNA is much more useful to further my research by identifying people with whom I match and comparing our paper documentation for clues to our connection. And DNA can solve some long-time family mysteries.

Tale of an adoptee

My cousin Justin always knew about his mother's twin siblings who the family thought had died shortly after they were born. But Justin's aunt found the lone scrap of paper that provided a clue to a twist in the story—torn-up adoption papers in a waste basket that gave the twins' names and birth date.

Adopted? It was a shock, but the family began to realize it made sense. Justin's grandmother had an unfortunate knack of choosing men who were alcoholic, abusive, or both. As a single, unemployed mom of five children in 1964, having two more children to care for after the twins were born must have been the final straw. Knowing she couldn't care for seven children, she gave up the twins for adoption.

The family began their 25-year search for the missing twins, but door after door seemed to slam shut as they hunted adoption agencies and worked their way through convoluted legal requirements, without even the help of the internet in the early years of their search. When DNA testing became available, Justin was excited that this might help their search and tested with the two companies with the biggest databases, hoping to find connections.

On the other side of this family puzzle was Amanda, who knew that her father and his twin sister had been adopted as babies. His adoptive parents were good people who fostered hundreds of children before adopting Amanda's father, aunt, and two other children. But Amanda's father was left bitter and angry, assuming that his biological parents hadn't wanted him or been ashamed somehow of his birth. Although he wanted no part of finding his biological family, Amanda was curious. She decided to take a DNA test.

Justin and Amanda matched as first cousins. Justin realized his family's 25-year search for his missing uncle and aunt had finally come to an end. Amanda was thrilled that her quest to find her father's biological family had succeeded. And her father, after learning the circumstances of why he was put up for adoption, found healing. (Unfortunately, his twin sister had already passed away in an accident.)

DNA can be the key to unlocking your family mysteries.

Unlocking Mysteries with DNA

DNA can be of value for everyone, not just for those wanting to solve adoption mysteries. For me, DNA is another tool in my genealogy toolkit, just like learning to read old German handwriting in old church records or discovering the family history possibilities of a KGB file.

I'm using DNA research in two ways—to supplement my paper documentation and to better understand the stories and migrations of different branches of the family. This opens up new possibilities for ancestral places to explore. (Although if I find any family members who were deported to the gulags, I might skip visiting Siberia.)

I have a good paper trail on most of my lines back to the 1700s (and earlier on some lines), but there are still those few that have weak or no paper trails. DNA can help find those branches of the family, either by confirming (or refuting) your weak paper trail or by connecting you with cousins that do have a paper trail to a common ancestor. DNA and record-based genealogy go hand in hand.

My family heritage is full of migrations—both voluntary and involuntary. When my three-times great-grandparents Jakob and Katharina (Kranzbuehler) Billigmeier left Germany for Imperial Russia (now Ukraine), some of their siblings and cousins stayed behind. When my four-times great-grandfather Johann Breitkreutz left Poland for Ukraine, siblings and cousins stayed behind in Poland. When my family left Ukraine to come to the U.S., some family members stayed behind or went to South America.

Each of these families followed a different path from my own direct line and had vastly different life experiences—from building up farms in Brazil to being shot or deported to Kazakhstan by the Soviets. Through DNA, I hope to connect with some of these distant family members and better understand their journeys, which is another branch of my family history.

How to use DNA for your research

I've just started my own journey with DNA genealogy, so I am far away from being an expert. There is a lot to learn. As I started to work on this myself, I felt like I was a genealogy newbie again, back when I didn't know a census record from an obituary. Sometimes the DNA journey felt overwhelming—much more difficult than it should be for the average person interested in family history. Some of the DNA-for-beginners articles I read or presentations I attended seem to be more biology class than introduction to a new method for researching genealogy.

So my goal is to help you understand some of the basics that I've learned. I don't want people stuck in the mode that I was, thinking, "Well, that was an interesting biology lesson, but what do I actually do with this? It feels impossible."

Which Type of DNA Test Should I Take?

There are three types of genealogy tests available: autosomal, Y DNA, and mtDNA.

Autosomal tests are the most popular, and these are the tests available from every testing service. Both men and women can take an autosomal test and learn something about their family on both their mother's and father's sides. The results will definitely connect you with third cousins and closer. You can also connect with more distant cousins (I recently connected with a seventh cousin), but after third cousins, the probability that you'll share DNA starts to decrease dramatically.

Autosomal tests analyze your 22 autosomal chromosome pairs (more on the biology behind all this in a minute). These tests identify the makeup of each chromosome, which then can be matched against other people's chromosomal makeup. When a segment of a specific chromosome matches that same segment/chromosome of another person, you are related.

Y DNA tests can only be taken by males, as only males have a Y chromosome. But a woman can take advantage of this test by having her father or brother test. (Or any paternal relative—your dad's brother or a male cousin on the paternal line of descent would also work.) This allows one to trace the family history of your father's father's father's father's line, which is typically the surname line. Y DNA tests work by identifying mutations (don't worry, nothing as dramatic as multiple heads) in the chromosome.

Let's say George has three sons named Tom, Dick, and Harry, and only Harry's Y chromosome has a small mutation. If you (or your father or brother) has that same mutation, you can confirm that you are descended from Harry, rather than Tom or Dick. Any other males who have that same mutation will also be related to you through Harry. But any distant cousins you find without the mutation must be descended from Tom or Dick.

Mitochondrial DNA (or mtDNA) tests can be taken by anyone, but are not that useful for genealogy purposes. The mtDNA test traces your mother's mother's mother's mother's line. Similar to Y DNA, analyzing mtDNA also works by tracking mutations. But because of how the DNA is passed down, the mutations happen so slowly with mtDNA that there's rarely anything new to learn in a genealogical time frame. It's interesting to know that my maternal line was in Dagestan 12,000 years ago, but that does not help me find the parents of Anna Greil (my three-times great-grandmother on my maternal line), who was born in 1809, probably in Prussia (which is a long way from Dagestan).

The biology of it all

Okay, let's go into the basics of the biology. You inherit half your DNA from your mom and half your DNA from your dad. That would lead you to believe that you inherit exactly 25 percent from each grandparent and 12.5 percent from each great-grandparent. Alas, it's not quite that simple.

In the heart (or nucleus) of each of the cells in our body, we have

22 chromosome pairs (called autosomes) plus one sex chromosome pair—23 chromosome pairs in all. Each of these 23 chromosome pairs consists of one chromosome you received from your mom and one you received from your dad.

(As an aside, many articles about DNA genealogy use the word chromosome to refer both to the 23 pairs of chromosomes *and* the individual chromosomes within each pair. Sometimes, they'll talk about different sides to a chromosome—maternal and paternal. All of this confused me hugely at first, so I'm hoping that talking about chromosome pairs, made up of one maternal chromosome and one paternal chromosome, will spare you that confusion. Because the difference matters when we start talking about matching DNA with distant cousins.)

So—you have 50 percent from your mom and 50 percent from your dad. Makes sense that you'd get 25 percent from each grandparent, because each of your parents has 50 percent of their DNA from each of their parents. But it doesn't work that way.

Picture the DNA you get from your mom as yellow and the DNA from your dad as green. You are half yellow and half green. Each of your parents is also half yellow and half green (from the DNA they got from their parents). But there's no guarantee that the DNA you get from your mom will come equally from her yellow half (your grandmother) and her green half (your grandfather). You might get 55 percent from her mom's (your grandmother's) yellow side and 45 percent from her dad's (your grandfather's) green side. As a result, instead of you having 25 percent from each of your maternal grandparents, you have 27.5 percent from your grandmother and 22.5 percent from your grandfather.

This can happen with each generation, so the amount of DNA you share with distant cousins varies quite a bit.

The 23rd chromosome pair (the sex chromosomes) is a bit more specialized than the autosomal chromosome pairs. The 23rd chromosome pair has two chromosomes (just like the autosomal chromosome pairs), and similarly, you inherit one chromosome from your dad and one from your mom. But men always inherit a Y chromosome from their dad and an X chromosome from their mom. Women have two X chromosomes in their sex chromosome pair—one that they received from their father and one from their mother. Because women have two X chromosomes and no Y chromosome, a Y DNA test can only be taken by a man.

When researching X-chromosome matches for a female, you don't know which chromosome in the pair she received from her father and which from her mother. But for a male, you know his X chromosome came from his mother.

And now for mtDNA. Each of our body's cells has these chromosomes we've been talking about, which are all included in the nucleus (or center) of the cell. Surrounding (but separate from) the nucleus in each cell is something called a mitochondrion.

These mitochondria also contain DNA—the mtDNA. This mtDNA is separate from the DNA in the 23 chromosomes in the nucleus. Because both men and women have mitochondria surrounding the nucleus of each of their cells, both men and women can test for mtDNA. But because both men and women get their mitochondria from their mothers, mtDNA always traces the mother's mother's mother's line. (The exact reason for why we don't inherit any mtDNA from our fathers seems to be up for research and discussion in the scientific community. But it's not important to get into for our purposes.)

However, mtDNA is not especially useful for genealogy purposes. The main comparison method is, like Y DNA, to identify different branches based on identifying specific mutations of the DNA. However, mutations occur much more slowly, less than once in every 100 people . . . which is a lot of great-grandmas.

Testing companies

With the spurt of popularity of DNA testing, testing companies seem to be popping up right and left. The advantage of this is that they're increasingly competitive (i.e., cheaper for you and me). The downside is that it's difficult to sort out which one to test with. As I write this, the big-name testing companies are FamilyTreeDNA, Ancestry, MyHeritage, and 23andMe. But the field is changing so fast that by the time you read this, there could be new players. For example, right now an up-and-coming (especially for those with British ancestry) testing company is LivingDNA.

If you're planning to be tested, most of these companies offer special pricing periodically—for Mother's Day, Father's Day, DNA Day (yes, that really is a thing).

In choosing which company to test with, a couple of the criteria to consider are size of their database (for maximizing the number of people with whom you match) and the tools available to research (such as chromosome browsers and availability of family trees). It also pays to be strategic. For example, you can pay to test at Ancestry, then upload those same results to FamilyTreeDNA for a small fee. This puts you in two databases at a lower price than doing two separate tests. (Currently, only FamilyTreeDNA and MyHeritage take uploads.)

This could all change next month the way the DNA genealogy field is changing, but here's my take on the big companies, based solely on my own experiences.

Ancestry

If you're hoping to connect with distant branches of the family, Ancestry has the biggest database, which makes a connection more likely. And because of Ancestry's focus on family history research, your match is more likely to have a family tree available to view. However, because Ancestry is so well known, many people who tested there did it only for the ethnicity results and aren't all that interested in genealogy. They may never log in again after viewing their results, which is very frustrating if they're the missing link in your research but never see your message. Also, Ancestry's lack of a chromosome browser limits some of the tools you can use.

MyHeritage

Although they're newer in the field than the others, I've experienced mostly awesomeness from using MyHeritage, although I have heard people mention problems with their software from time to time. Their interface and tools for researching matches are excellent, and more people from Europe seem to be testing there, which is helping me connect with distant cousins in Germany. They also seem to be good at listening to their customers' requests and feedback. However, for me, their ethnicity estimates were the most inaccurate.

FamilyTreeDNA

This company is, in some ways, the granddaddy of testing companies as they were one of the first of the companies to offer tests that is still in existence. They're the only company currently offering a complete spectrum of tests—autosomal, Y, and mtDNA. They also provide excellent tools for researching your matches. Since the people that use FamilyTreeDNA tend to be focused on genealogy, you tend to get responses when you send messages to your matches.

23andMe

This company had the biggest database for many years, but that seems to have dropped off. (I haven't been alerted to new matches there in quite a while). Their tools for researching matches seem very clumsy to me. But their ethnicity results are reasonably accurate, and they offer some health results.

Amazing Tools for Analyzing DNA

The existence of numerous testing companies is great for competition and reduced prices for all of us. But multiple testing companies create a challenge when you need to compare genetic relatives who have tested in different places.

Fortunately, some avid genealogists have created tools that allow you to compare your DNA matches regardless of where they've tested. I'll just talk about the two that I've used—GEDmatch and DNA Painter—although there are many more available and more springing up every day.

GEDmatch (www.gedmatch.com) is sometimes talked about in the same breath with the testing services. But they don't provide testing. Instead, this website is actually an online tool that allows you to upload your raw DNA results (from any testing company) and provides sophisticated methods for analyzing your matches, regardless of where they had their DNA tested. GEDmatch includes many tools that are available for free, with some of the more complex tools requiring a small fee for Tier 1 membership.

Some of GEDmatch's options include:

- A function to find out if your parents were related (important if your ancestors lived in communities with many intermarriages)
- The ability to analyze your ethnicity using tools/algorithms that are designed for specific ethnic groups and which may be more representative of your heritage than the standard algorithm each testing company has created
- The ability to phase your data (that is, separate what you received from your mother versus your father), although you need results from at least one parent for this to work
- The Lazarus tool, which allows you to re-create the DNA of someone (such as a parent or grandparent) who isn't available to test by using the DNA from closely related people such as siblings or cousins

GEDmatch is a DNA data geek's Disneyland.

As for DNA Painter (https://dnapainter.com), I have absolutely fallen in love with this tool. When I first tip-toed into the waters of DNA genealogy a few years ago, this was the tool I wanted and didn't even know it until it appeared. I was trying to do something complicated with spreadsheets to compare matching segments for DNA matches I found in different testing companies' databases. It became such a complicated mess that I couldn't figure it out (even though I'd created it), and I sort of lost my interest in DNA genealogy for a while.

DNA Painter allows you to compare matches across testing companies in a visual way that also breaks out your known matches by the maternal and paternal sides. This was incredibly exciting to me. Because both of my parents are gone, I can't test either one to separate out which chromosome in each pair I got from which parent. But in DNA Painter, when I identify a match with someone and discover our common ancestor based on the paper record, I can assign that match to either the paternal or maternal chromosome for each pair.

This is huge for me, because it helps me narrow down the possibilities of which family line to search for new matches. I also love the visual approach of DNA Painter, which I find much easier to work with than tons of spreadsheets. And being able to track matches regardless of their testing company is much simpler than contacting all these individuals and persuading them to upload their results to another database or to GEDmatch so I can compare them.

A sample of my DNA matches, "painted" in DNA Painter. I'm using darker colors (blues, greens) for my paternal side and lighter colors (pinks, yellows) for my maternal side.
(Image courtesy of DNA Painter)

Analyzing Your DNA

I remember the first time I looked at a list of my DNA matches. Because I had no idea of where to start, I basically panicked. I didn't see surnames I recognized and didn't know what other step to take, so I just logged out. Experimenting with DNA Painter, GEDmatch, and the tools available in each of the places I've tested has helped me become more systematic about working through my matches to identify our most common recent ancestor (MCRA) where possible, and then use DNA Painter to document my matches and compare with matches from other testing companies.

I am admittedly still a beginner in DNA research, and I'm sure there are many other approaches to take, but here are a few simple steps that have worked for me in analyzing my autosomal DNA results.

Check the relationship distance

All the testing companies show your DNA matches listed in order of how close your probable relationship is, measured in centiMorgans (cMs), which is just a measurement of DNA. You share about 3,487 cMs of DNA with each parent. You share about 2,209 to 3,384 cMs with each of your siblings. (Each of you inherits 50 percent of your DNA from each parent, but you each inherit different parts of each parent's DNA so you're not going to exactly match your sibling's DNA.)

As relationships get more distant, the amount of DNA you share becomes correspondingly less. The probability that you'll share any DNA at all also decreases. For third cousins, there's a 90 percent chance the two of you will share DNA, and on average, you'll share 74 cMs of DNA (though the amount shared can range from 0 to 217 cMs). But for fourth cousins, there's only a 50 percent chance you'll share DNA at all, and it will average 35 cMs (with a range of 0 to 127 cMs).

The chances of sharing DNA with more distant cousins are even lower. There's only about a 10 percent chance of sharing DNA with a fifth cousin, and the probability gets miniscule after that. Still, it's possible to hit the jackpot as I've recently connected with a seventh cousin with whom I share 20 cM of DNA.

The first time I ran into a situation in which I didn't share any DNA with a documented fourth cousin, I suspected an NPE (not parent expected or non-paternity event). It was a conundrum because his family resemblance to my grandfather is strong, making an NPE unlikely. But as I've learned more about DNA, I've realized that the law of probabilities is likely to be the culprit.

At more distant levels of relationships, you can have genealogical cousins (people who are descended from the same ancestors as you are) who aren't genetic cousins (people who you share DNA with). The reverse, however, is not true. If you share DNA with someone, you are genealogical cousins somehow, even if you don't have the documentation to understand it.

One exception is that, in general, if you share less than 7 cM of DNA with someone, that is most often a false positive, or in other words, a bit of DNA that is common enough to general populations that you could share it without also being genealogical cousins.

As you review matches, each testing company will provide an estimate of your relationship with that person, but I've found the estimates provided by the Shared cM Project to be the most accurate: https://dnapainter.com/tools/sharedcm.

Check your match's family tree

Once I identify a match, I try to identify how we're related by checking for their family tree. GEDmatch and all testing companies (except 23andMe) allow you to upload a tree to go along with your DNA, though not everyone does. If I don't see a tree associated with my match's DNA, I also check if my match has a tree in Ancestry or MyHeritage, as some people have online trees that they haven't connected to their DNA results in their testing company.

Even if your match has a family tree, you may not find obvious connections, depending on how far back in time each of you has a paper trail on your family. If I can't find a connection through a family tree (or can't find a family tree), I'll start comparing who else shares our DNA.

Comparing matches

Here's where I think it gets a bit tricky. Let's say "Sue" pops up on my list of DNA matches. My first step is to see who else matches both Sue and me.

It's tempting to look at the list of matches we share and think "Wow, all of us are related!" But it's not quite that simple. I might match Sue through my paternal grandmother. I might match Joe through my maternal grandmother. Sue and Joe might match each other through some completely different family line. Even if it appears that Sue and Joe and I all match at the same location on my chromosome pair, it doesn't mean that we all descend from the same ancestor. Sue and I might match in that location on my paternal chromosome at the same location that Joe and I match on the maternal chromosome of that chromosome pair.

The only way to be sure that we all descend from the same ancestor is to triangulate my matches with Sue and Joe, which shows that

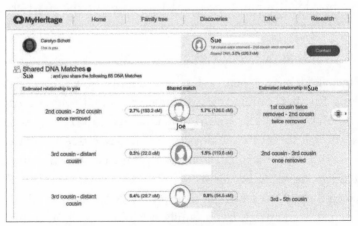

(Image courtesy of MyHeritage)

all three of us actually match on the exact same chromosome. Each testing company has different ways of displaying data, but I'll show you an example from MyHeritage.

The screen shot on the previous page shows all the matches I share with Sue. The little symbol on the right shows that Sue and Joe and I triangulate. When I click on that icon, it shows me the segment of DNA that we all share, giving me assurance that we're all related. Now we just need to compare family trees to determine where.

The other matches on this list show that I share a common ancestor with them, as does Sue, but we may not be descended from the same ancestor.

Tracking your matches

I'm using DNA Painter as my central tracking tool as it allows me to enter matches that I've discovered at GEDmatch or any of the testing companies. It also gives me the ability to separate matches into my paternal and maternal sides, which I do based on my paper trail once I've confirmed the connection.

Some people paint (i.e., document them in DNA Painter) all their matches, but I've generally only painted the ones that I can track to a common ancestor or at least to a specific family line. My goal is to create a profile with as many known matches as I can find and then use that to help track down the family lines for unknown matches.

As I research an unknown match, I overlay that match onto my current profile in DNA Painter to see if there are known, painted matches that match the unknown one I'm researching. If it looks like there is a possibility of a match, I can go into the testing site to do further research and comparison. Or if the two matches tested at different companies, I can contact one or both of my matches to ask them to upload their results somewhere where all three of us can compare.

For example, I recently matched H. through MyHeritage, and we can't figure out where our family lines connect. But on DNA Painter, I could see that the DNA segments we share overlap with C., a match from my fathers's side whose DNA is in FamilyTreeDNA and GEDmatch, and also overlaps with K., a match from my mother's side whose DNA is in 23andMe. I've asked H. if he would upload his MyHeritage results into either FamilyTreeDNA or GEDmatch (which both allow transfers) so I could see if he matches C. If he doesn't match C., the connection between H. and me is most likely on my mother's side.

I also put notes on each of my matches (using the notes feature provided by each testing company) stating that I've painted the match or that I've contacted the person for more information and to document what I discover about our common ancestry. The cardinal rule of genealogy—always document what you've done.

Shared matches on Ancestry

I haven't worked with Ancestry as much as the other companies because my reliance on DNA Painter (which requires specific start/stop points of chromosome segments) is incompatible with Ancestry's lack of a chromosome browser that provides this data.

However, with so many people testing with Ancestry, there is definitely value to working your matches there using their DNA Match tool. Their DNA Circles tool, which combines analysis of your family tree to your DNA matches to identify possible common ancestors, is also useful. This recently helped me find evidence that I have correctly identified the parents of my great-great-grandmother, Katharina Bohlander, even though my paper trail is weak.

Ancestry continues to add new tools all the time, which will be invaluable in making the most of this huge database.

Other tools and looking forward

There are lots of other tools and techniques that you can use to solve the relationship puzzles that your DNA reveals. The ones I've described are what I'm using personally, but new ideas keep coming up every day. If you want to find out more about how to analyze your

DNA, see the list of resources I've provided at the end of the chapter.

However, I know that I was overwhelmed when I started my DNA journey and would have found some of these basics helpful rather than stumbling around trying to figure things out as I did. So I hope this overview was useful to get you started.

Privacy

You may be considering testing and wondering about privacy concerns. Or you may be trying to persuade a relative to test, and they have concerns about the use of their DNA. But no matter how desperately you need their results to fill in family gaps, don't forget that others may not share your passion for uncovering family connections, and they have the right to be private with their DNA if that's what they want.

Of course, it's certainly appropriate to persuasively provide data that would help calm their concerns. And it's certainly appropriate to explain what an important legacy they are leaving to their family by having their DNA tested. And okay, I admit it, I wouldn't be above begging them, with family historian desperation in my voice.

Just to give you a start, here are some of the things that people often express concern about before agreeing to a DNA test.

One person told me that they were worried that if a testing company had their DNA, they could create a clone of that person. However, the amount of DNA that is tested for genealogical purposes is not enough to create a clone. So I am not at all worried about a "mini me" running around without my knowledge. And really, even if a DNA genealogy test could be used to clone someone, I think if anyone was going to go to all that trouble, they'd clone someone brilliant like Stephen Hawking or Ruth Bader Ginsburg before cloning me. (Not to disparage myself, but even on my best days, I'm not as brilliant as Stephen or as tough as Ruth.)

Another fear is that people often think testing companies own your data after you send it to them. That is not true. Read their terms and conditions.

Others are nervous because they fear that testing companies can do whatever they want with your data. Well, their terms and conditions do include you granting them the right to use your data, but that is a basic requirement for them to be able to analyze your sample and compare it with others in the database—which is the whole purpose for you doing the test in the first place.

The 2018 capture of the Golden State Killer using a DNA genealogy website (and a number of other solved cold cases since then) caused another round of concern about how DNA data can be used. However, the website that was used in this case clearly states in its terms and conditions that, although the purpose of the database is for genealogy, they could not prevent the data from being used for other purposes. Since this case broke, they've added more explicit warning notices and require you to acknowledge this risk before uploading your data.

Personally, I'm okay if my data is used to help lock up a murderer and rapist. But admittedly, it is the proverbial slippery slope. If law enforcement uses genealogy databases today for solving murders and rapes, will they use it tomorrow to solve lesser crimes that each of us individually may not be so supportive of contributing to?

There is sometimes concern that your DNA data will be used to discriminate against you, but in the U.S., there is a federal law prohibiting discrimination in employment and health insurance. Life insurance may not have equal protection, however, so that would be one thing to consider. Of course, laws change, and this is one of those potential slippery slope areas that could come up in the future. If this is an area of concern for you, it's worthwhile to do additional reading on the topic.

DNA data is personal, but each of us shares personal data in numerous ways every day. If you use Facebook or buy things with a credit card or apply to rent an apartment, personal information about where you are, what you own, and your financial history is in numerous databases already. It can be useful to mention this to a relative expressing concern and ask why doing a DNA test concerns them more than some of these common ways we manage our lives in the 21st century.

The risk that rarely seems to come up, however, is actually the one most likely to occur—finding out that you or another relative is not who they thought they were. DNA has a way of uncovering family secrets—the baby given up for adoption or an extramarital affair that produced a child—that was hidden until now. In the genetic genealogy groups I follow, this is the situation that comes up on pretty much a daily basis, not any of the other concerns I mentioned. This is a risk each of us must be prepared for when submitting our DNA for analysis.

If you are talking to a relative about doing a DNA test, you should be sure they understand the actual risks, in addition to emphasizing the importance of leaving this legacy to the family. You should talk with them ahead of time about whether they want you to tell them if you discover a family secret or if they'd prefer not to know.

In some cases, you might be in the position that your relative agrees to take the test but doesn't want to deal with managing their information or respond to matches' messages. All testing companies will allow your relative to designate you as the administrator or manager of their data. In this situation, it is also good to ask your relative in advance if they will allow you to upload their data to other sites to enhance the research options. The more conversation you have upfront about some of these issues, the less likely there will be unpleasant surprises later.

Personally, I recognize and have considered the risk of all these concerns. But for me, the benefit of connecting with distant relatives, and uncovering the story of branches of the family that I would never have known about, far outweighs the potential problems.

For more thoughts on DNA genealogy privacy concerns, read The Legal Genealogist: www.legalgenealogist.com/2017/05/21/with-all-due-respect/

Additional Resources on DNA Genealogy

This chapter has just scratched the surface of what there is to learn about researching your ancestors through DNA. I hope it gives you enough information to get started on your exploration and provides a foundation for learning more. As you dive deeper, the resources I would recommend are:

- *The Family Tree Guide to DNA Testing and Genetic Genealogy* by Blaine T. Bettinger. This is a must read to get a deeper understanding of how DNA works and using it for research. I took a DNA workshop from Blaine and walked out thinking, "At last! Someone who speaks English and can explain this without making my head spin!"

- The *Genetic Genealogist* blog (https://thegeneticgenealogist.com) by Blaine. A great way to keep up to date on new happenings in the DNA genealogy field.

- The *DNAeXplained* blog (https://dna-explained.com) by Roberta Estes. Another great blog that explains DNA genealogy in understandable language.

- Genetic Genealogy Tips and Techniques Facebook group (www.facebook.com/groups/geneticgenealogytipsandtechniques). This is a helpful group of genealogy researchers who are incredibly supportive about answering questions. They're even patient when different people ask multiple times per day the very vague question, "How do I get started?" But you won't have to ask that, as you've just read this book!

- The International Society of Genetic Genealogy (https://isogg.org). This is the granddaddy of all DNA genealogy websites. Lots of helpful information on their website, which will go into great depth about using DNA for your research.

- "Mapping Your Chromosomes with DNA Painter" by Blaine Bettinger (www.youtube.com/watch?v=wyjcJxywTZI). This is a step-by-step video guide to getting started with DNA Painter.

Location	Documen-tation	23andMe	FTDNA	Ancestry	GEDMatch	Nat Geo	My Heritage
Specific matches:							
German	100.0%						
French & German		25.5%					
General matches:							
General European		10.1%					
West/central Europe			31.0%	48.0%		24.0%	
North/west Europe		35.2%					
North Atlantic					39.2%		
Baltic					31.0%		
Speculative matches:							
General Eastern Europe		23.2%	55.0%	32.0%		39.0%	5.8%
Non-matches							
Scandinavian		0.6%	12.0%	4.0%		18.0%	32.2%
English				6.0%			7.7%
British & Irish		3.3%					
Southern European		0.8%		1.0%		14.0%	
Balkan		0.9%					54.3%
West/East Mediterranean					22.7%		
Iberian				7.0%			
Finnish			2.0%	1.0%		3.0%	
Siberian					2.0%		
Red Sea					0.8%		
Asia Minor/Caucasus				1.0%		2.0%	
West Asian					4.2%		
East Asian/Native American		0.1%					
Oceanian					0.1%		
Sub-Saharan Africa		0.2%					
Total	100.0%	99.9%	100.0%	100.0%	100.0%	100.0%	100.0%

A comparison of my documented heritage with ethnicity estimates from DNA testing companies as of February 2018.

In Their Footsteps

Dabbling in DNA
(Original blog post: February 27, 2018, updated October 2018)

You may have seen the Ancestry ad where a man trades in his lederhosen for a kilt after taking a DNA test that shows he is more Scottish than German.

A word of warning—if you make your wardrobe choices based on a DNA test, you may want to make sure that store takes returns. And if you plan your travel to ancestral lands that way, well, let's just say that you should buy a refundable airline ticket. DNA ethnicity estimates are just that—estimates.

But "DNA is science," you might argue. "It has to be right." It's true that the actual DNA is a biological certainty, and there are ways that DNA can be used for genealogy that are scientifically accurate. But ethnicity estimates are in the educated guess category.

As a genealogy nerd, I've tested with or uploaded my results to six different DNA testing firms or tools. Just for fun, I've been dabbling with comparing these six ethnicity estimates to my actual heritage, which I can document as 100 percent ethnic German to all 32 of my three-times great-grandparents (which takes me into the 1700s), to the 28 of 64 four-times great-grandparents that I've identified, and to my 6X great-grandparents (about 1600s) on several lines.

Out of all these tests, only one (23andMe) identified a chunk of my DNA as specifically German (or at least, German/French). Most of the tests DO correctly (but vaguely) identify large chunks of my DNA as European (north, west, central). I also think the North Atlantic and Baltic categories that GEDmatch uses make sense, as I'm fairly certain a number of my lines started out in the northeastern part of Germany that borders or is now Poland.

The numbers that look stranger to me are the high percentages in Eastern Europe and the Balkans. My peeps lived in these regions but came from Germany and intermarried with other Germans. When I first saw these large amounts, I suspected an NPE (non-paternity event, aka a biological father that doesn't match the documented German father I have in my records). But as I learn more, I think these unexpected results are just as likely (probably more likely) to be a symptom of the estimating process than an illicit affair by one of my ancestresses.

The testing process

First, the testing companies use reference populations from their databases to estimate ethnicities. The people used for these reference populations are chosen because they appear to have deep roots in a particular area. My results are influenced by who has tested with any particular company and who the company has chosen to use as their reference population.

As far as I know, I'm not a reference population person. But if I were, I have many generations of ancestors born in Poland and Ukraine. Anyone in the reference population who looks like me would indeed appear to be Eastern European, despite the original German roots.

You also have to look at each testing company's definition of their geographic areas. Ancestry shows me as 6 percent British, but their definition of Great Britain includes part of the European mainland, right around France/Netherlands/Germany where my ancestors could have been roaming around.

My specific heritage also highlights the issue of migrations and how difficult it is to pinpoint where a person came from, especially within a geographically contiguous area like Europe. (And don't fool yourself, despite the lack of cars/trains/planes, our ancestors wandered around a lot—just more slowly.)

My heritage is German, despite the generations my family spent in Ukraine, Poland, and Hungary. Of course, I have no idea where my family members were in the 1200s. Maybe they were in Great Britain getting ready to migrate to Germany, or part of Genghis Khan's raiding parties heading west toward Germany. Prior to the 1600s, my ancestors might well have been somewhere other than Germany.

How to use DNA to sort this out

Bottom line—the ethnicity estimates are a lot of fun. They're a great first step into exploring your genetic genealogy. But don't expect this to provide significant clues to your family history.

Where DNA is helpful is by using it to identify distant cousins with whom you share DNA and comparing your documented family history to theirs to find out new clues about your ancestors. You may discover some three-times great-grandparents that you can't find documentation on, but your distant cousin has. You may discover that branches of your family wandered places that you never knew about. (I suspect some branches of my family ended up in Siberia or Kazakhstan, but I don't have documentation on that.)

Best way to get started is: (1) take a DNA test, (2) load it into GED-match, (3) buy Blaine Bettinger's book *The Family Tree Guide to DNA Testing and Genetic Genealogy*. (I took a DNA workshop from Blaine once. He is awesome in his knowledge.) GEDmatch has tons of free tools to analyze your DNA, and Blaine's book will tell you how to make use of those tools most effectively.

Then—go forth and use real science to uncover the power of DNA.

Update: October 2018

Since I wrote this original blog post, both 23andMe and Ancestry have updated their ethnicity algorithms to make them more accurate, so I reviewed my results to see how much they'd changed.

My 23andMe estimate didn't change at all, but my Ancestry estimate changed quite a lot. They are the testing company that is now most accurate, showing me as 60 percent German (versus my 100 percent German heritage documented).

Although the details change, my message stays the same: ethnicity estimates are fun but are still just estimates.

Location	Documentation	23andMe	FTDNA	Ancestry	GEDMatch	Nat Geo	My Heritage
Specific matches:							
German	100.0%			60.0%			
French & German		25.5%					
General matches:							
General European		10.1%					
West/central Europe			31.0%			24.0%	
North/west Europe		35.2%					
North Atlantic					39.2%		
Baltic					31.0%		
Speculative matches:							
General Eastern Europe		23.2%	55.0%	21.0%		39.0%	5.8%
Non-matches:							
Scandinavian		0.6%	12.0%	18.0%		18.0%	32.2%
English			1.0%				7.7%
British & Irish		3.3%					
Southern European		0.8%				14.0%	
Balkan		0.9%					54.3%
West/East Mediterranean					22.7%		
Iberian							
Finnish			2.0%			3.0%	
Siberian					2.0%		
Red Sea					0.8%		
Asia Minor/Caucasus						2.0%	
West Asian					4.2%		
East Asian/Native American		0.1%					
Oceanian					0.1%		
Sub-Saharan Africa		0.2%					
Total	100.0%	99.9%	100.0%	100.0%	100.0%	100.0%	100.0%

My ethnicity estimates using updated estimates
from 23andMe and Ancestry.

Chapter 5

Locating Your Ancestral Town

Looking at a map with residents of
Benkendorf (Velykomar'yanivka), Ukraine

Searching the Globe

Once you've researched your ancestors to find where they came from—whether through online records, paper records, or DNA—you're probably ready to look on the map for where all those ancestral places are.

If your ancestral town is nearby or you have specific information about it, this may be as simple as looking at a road map or online map. Even if I hadn't traveled to my parents' birthplace of Kulm every year as a child, it pops up easily on a map of North Dakota. No problem at all finding it.

But when I looked for my grandparents' birthplaces of Hoffnungstal and Gnadenfeld in "South Russia," I had a much more difficult time. South Russia is not a specific, recognizable geographic region. The area where my grandparents lived is currently in the country of Ukraine. However, when I search the term South Russia now, the results come back as an area in current-day Russia, far from where these villages actually are.

These were ethnic German villages from the 19th through the mid-20th centuries. Hoffnungstal has been destroyed, although it is still labeled on maps of Ukraine as a ghost town named Nadezhdivka. Gnadenfeld still exists but is known only by its Ukrainian name of Blahodatne. Therefore, looking for either of these villages by their German names on a current map doesn't help me.

Another complication, even after I found information on ethnic German villages in modern-day Ukraine, was that there were multiple villages with the names Hoffnungstal and Gnadenfeld. Gnadenfeld was especially problematic because my grandmother's Gnadenfeld was very small with little information available about it. Another Gnadenfeld, which is much larger, was mentioned in every reference I looked at, but my grandmother's Gnadenfeld was difficult to find.

When there are multiple possibilities for your ancestral town or other uncertainties about its location, be sure to be thorough in your research so you pin down the right one.

Maps

My first instinct these days is to look at Google Maps. And although this is a great resource, it doesn't reliably find every town. It steadfastly refuses to find my Billigmeier family's hometown of Gräfenhausen, near Annweiler, Germany. (I first located that Gräfenhausen using Expedia maps—which apparently no longer exists.) Google Maps also may not recognize a smaller town that has been incorporated into a larger town.

In that case, you'll need to branch out. A great source of links to online maps is on Cyndi's List (www.cyndislist.com/maps). Other great sources are gazetteers (geographical dictionaries) or atlases.

These can generally be found in genealogy libraries (such as your local Family History Center) or local libraries near where your ancestors lived. Historical maps that date from the time your ancestors lived there can provide state and county boundaries and may help you locate the nearest church or office where vital records were kept.

There are also online gazetteers. Ancestry has a number of gazetteers online (at least some of which are available without a subscription). Search the card catalog under "Maps, Atlases & Gazetteers." One great gazetteer I use for locations in Germany is gov.genealogy. net/index.jsp.

But my all-time favorite gazetteer for Germany is the *Meyers Gazetteer*, which is online at www.meyersgaz.org. It was compiled in 1912 at the height of the German Empire, which means it covers a large territory, including many areas no longer part of Germany. It's long been the "go to" source for finding small towns in Germany as it was published before most of these small towns were swallowed up by bigger cities.

The original book form was an awesome reference, but you had to decipher the old-style Fraktur font. The online version is an amazing tool, providing the locations of nearby religious and civil offices (where you might find records), as well as options for historical and current maps. For more on using the online *Meyers Gazetteer*, see my blog post: www.carolynschott.com/germany/fun-with-the-meyers-gazetteer.

Genealogy organizations

Genealogy organizations focusing on your ethnic background or geographic area can be a great source of information. Being a member of an organization that focuses on ethnic Germans in Russia helped me find the locations of Gnadenfeld and Hoffnungstal. This organization had a number of reference books, maps, webpages, and knowledgeable people who helped me figure out the correct locations of these villages. Joining an organization on Scottish heritage led my friend Jane to detailed information about the clan her family came from.

Finding a website about ethnic Germans in Hungary and participating in the Listserv for that group was the key to finding out that Jenk was really Gyönk and where it is located. Networking with genealogists who know about your area can be one of the best ways to find your village.

Checking the Location

If you have multiple possibilities for your ancestral town or there is any uncertainty about the location you think you've identified, you'll want to confirm you have the right town before planning a trip there. The most certain way to do this is to find birth, marriage, or death records for your ancestor in that town. But if that's not possible, there are other ways to confirm the location.

Even though I couldn't find my grandmother's birth record, I had a pretty good idea which of the multiple villages called Gnadenfeld was her hometown. I knew that most of the people in the area of North Dakota where my grandmother lived had come from an area called Bessarabia, so the Gnadenfeld in Bessarabia was most likely my ancestral town. I was able to confirm this by finding a book on Gnadenfeld, Bessarabia, that listed my great-grandparents as founders of the village.

The best ways to confirm your location are:
- Birth, marriage, or death records. Church records are usually the best source.
- Other information that is specific to the town that might list the residents, such as town histories, census lists, tax lists, etc.
- The name of your village may contain a reference that will help you. Frankfurt am Main and Frankfurt an der Oder are two very different places. The reference to the river they are near (the Main or the Oder) helps distinguish them.

- Knowing some of the history about these places may help. I knew my grandmother lived in an area settled by people from Bessarabia. I also knew that she was Protestant. So the Gnadenfeld in Bessarabia, which was a Protestant (Lutheran) village, was much more likely to be her birthplace than the Gnadenfeld in the Taurien area that had been settled by Mennonites.
- Sometimes looking at town information and not finding your ancestor's name is a clue. I searched through many records for Oberkleen, Germany, where I was sure my Schott family was from, but could not find any Schotts. Not finding them on the tax lists encouraged me to search further (because surely, if any lists would be complete, it would be the lists used to collect taxes!), and I found them in Ober-Gleen, Germany.

Using printed translations from Google, I attempt to communicate with workmen on the streets of Kochanów, Poland.

In Their Footsteps

In Search of an Elusive Ancestral Town
(Original blog post: March 14, 2014)

Dripping blood, missing rental car, taxi careening through traffic—as I told the rental car agency guy (when we finally found him), "We've had a hard time leaving Warsaw this morning."

Once we were on the road though, things proceeded smoothly. Roads were clearly marked and matched my maps from Google. We drove straight to my first ancestral town, Kochanów (or Erdmannsweiler, as it was called by the German settlers), where my Brenner and Zaiser families lived for a generation in about 1800. It was a pleasant town of well-kept, updated homes. We met a friendly construction guy who clearly was intrigued by the paper of Polish translations I thrust in front of him. (My name is Carolyn. My ancestors came from this village. Do you know where the old German cemetery is?) He directed us to the cemetery and hooked us up with a local who regretfully indicated that there were no 200-year-old houses in town.

Although I found no specific traces of my long-gone ancestors (not even old German headstones), it was a pleasant visit to a pleasant town. The flat lands of Ukraine and North Dakota, where my ancestors later settled, must have seemed very familiar to them after the flat lands of Poland. And we saw the Catholic church in the nearby town of Gluchow, which would have been the civil registration place for the births, marriages, and deaths of my Lutheran ancestors before there was a Lutheran church in town.

My two nongenealogy friends had only signed up for one ancestral town. But they agreed to visit a second when I assured them the next town on my list was just up the road a few kilometers, on our way, and just five minutes off the road.

An hour later, we were still searching for Boginia as we turned onto a narrow road between small lakes, then plunged into the woods as we bounced over a spine-wrenching, rutted road. The road that had been "on our way" and seemingly clearly marked had been the wrong road.

"Turn here, no wait, here. Wait, I think we've gone too far," I said, trying to navigate an alternate route to my ancestral town of Boginia. I finally turned on my smartphone and GPS (I'd been holding off, rationing data usage on my global plan) to figure out which rutted road most likely led to our destination.

We finally burst out of the woods back onto a paved road bordering fields, then entered Boginia (a town of no more than about 20 houses) through its "suburbs." The setting was pretty—rolling hills, woods, small lakes, farmhouses dotted here and there. Yet there was no town at all (the distance between the "entering Boginia" sign and the "leaving Boginia" sign could have been walked in less than five minutes and included only about two buildings).

I stopped a man on a tractor who read my paper of Polish explanations, then shook his head and handed it back, looking sorry he'd stopped. Another man in a car avoided my eyes and wouldn't stop at all. (Even though I was standing in his driveway taking photos; you'd think he would at least have been curious.) Apparently, no church, no cemetery, no recognition of a history of German settlers.

My Breitkreutz family has always been elusive and their (possible) ancestral town of Boginia proved to be equally elusive. I'd hoped our convoluted search for the town would be rewarded with the discovery of an overgrown cemetery filled with German headstones or a crumbling 200-year-old house, but alas.

Sometimes the adventure of the search is more interesting than the destination.

Chapter 6

Planning Your Trip

*The village of Queichhambach, Germany, where I discovered my
ancestors went to church, although they lived in another village.*

How to Prepare for a Successful Trip

Now that you've located your ancestral town, it's time to start planning the details of your trip. You'll need to make the standard travel plans any traveler makes—airlines, rental cars, rail passes, and hotels. But you'll also need to make plans specific to visiting your ancestral town.

By spending more time researching and making contacts before you leave, you'll have a better chance of seeing more places specific to your interests while you're there.

Different ways to plan your trip

You can plan your trip using a standard tour group, a specialty tour group, or by making your own arrangements independently. Each has pros and cons.

A standard tour group is the easiest travel experience to plan since the tour agent will generally make all the arrangements. This is the best option if you don't have time for or aren't comfortable making your own arrangements. Although this method is unlikely to give you the opportunity to visit a specific ancestral town, you'll get a good sense of the country or culture without worrying about travel planning or navigating in an unfamiliar place.

Some tour agencies specialize in heritage tours to locations specific to family history and genealogy interests. Using one of these agencies to visit your ancestral town can give you the benefit of having someone else do most of the work to organize the trip.

A tour operator might be able to customize a tour just for you and your family (although this could be expensive depending on the size of your group), or you may travel with a group that shares similar interests. In that case, you need to be prepared that the travel time will be split between your own ancestral towns and that of others in the group.

Traveling independently gives you the most flexibility if you are comfortable taking on the travel planning yourself. But this option also takes the most time in advance.

I've used all these methods at one time or another. It's important to plan a trip that is comfortable for you and your group, balancing how much work you want to do with how many specific locations you will be able to visit.

Things to consider when making travel plans

Finding your comfort level

If you're merely driving across the state to visit your parent's hometown for the first time, you probably have a pretty good idea how to get there and find your way around. If you're a seasoned traveler, even if you're going to a new location, you may also feel pretty comfortable navigating your way and making your own travel plans.

But if you're going to another country for the first time or to a culture very different from your own, or if you haven't had much experience traveling, you may want to have someone else do all or most of the trip planning, as well as guiding you while you're there.

You'll also want to think about your travel companions and their comfort level with the travel arrangements. Even if you're such a seasoned traveler that you're comfortable arriving in a country and making arrangements on the fly, that might be too stressful for your elderly mother or cautious brother traveling with you.

Prepare for local conditions

It's a good idea to get an understanding of local conditions at your destination so unpleasant surprises don't negatively influence your trip. When my cousin-in-law visited her father's hometown in Cambodia, her parents warned her about the lack of electricity, lack of running water, and squat toilets in a shed. Knowing this in advance helped my cousin-in-law mentally prepare, so she could take the basic accommodations in stride. Her advance knowledge paved the way and allowed her to enjoy the family connections she was making rather than being distracted by the living conditions.

What are your trip deal breakers?

Before you start planning, it's good to understand what is most important to experience on your trip. What are your deal breakers, the places or experiences that, if you missed them, would leave you feeling you'd wasted your trip?

Is it the church where your grandparents were married? A specific house or cemetery? Are you happy with whatever you might see? Or do you just want to get a glimpse of the culture? Are you a genealogist hoping to do research while on your travels? Are you trying to meet distant relatives?

Your specific goals will help determine the type of travel planning that is best for you.

If your main goal is to experience the culture, your preparation will be similar to any other traveler, ranging from making the travel arrangements to reading up on the general history and sights of the area you're visiting.

If you want to stroll through your ancestor's town, you'll at least need to locate where it is and find out how to get there. You may also want to do a little background reading about that town.

If you have some very specific places you want to see in your ancestral town (e.g., your great-grandparents' home, a cemetery in a hard-to-find location), you'll want to do more work ahead of time. Is there a family member who can take you there or give you directions to find the place on your own? Is there a visitors' bureau? In a smaller town, you might write or email the town mayor or town council, the pastor of a church, or the person in charge of a local museum.

There's also research you can do on your own. This can range from looking up addresses and searching online for a location, to looking up old Bureau of Land Management (BLM) township maps, to looking at plat maps of foreign villages. If your ancestors lived in a city, like New York or Stockholm, it can actually be more problematic to find specific houses or buildings (which may have been redeveloped over the years) so more digging is needed.

On a recent visit to North Dakota, I decided to visit the country cemetery where my great-grandfather and great-great-grandmother are buried. I'd been there before but always with one of my local relatives who knew their way around the gravel section line roads. This time, a friend and I ventured out with the BLM township maps as our main guide. This meant veering off the county highway onto gravel roads, hoping we'd read the map right as we traveled through acres and acres of farmland with no other landmarks in sight.

Fortunately, due to a national emergency preparedness initiative, there are now city-style rural road signs at each section line crossing.

This made it a bit easier for a city girl like me to find a country cemetery that is miles from any town. And we only went down one wrong road! (It seemed like a good idea at the time to take the shortest route back to the main county road, but it was a mud pit.)

The one disappointment of this excursion was that I hadn't prepared a bit more. When I got home, I realized the country school both of my parents had taught at used to be almost directly across the gravel road from this cemetery. Even though I know the schoolhouse is gone, it would have been fun to look more closely at the spot where it had been located.

On a trip to Ukraine, I went to much more elaborate lengths to find the house where my ancestors had lived, even though the house no longer exists. After the ethnic German villagers (including my grandfather's brothers' families) left in 1940, a military base on an overlooking hill had used the empty houses for target practice. All had been destroyed.

Even though I knew this when I went to Ukraine, I still came prepared with a map of the village. Although the houses were gone, the overgrown rubble of each of the homes created regularly spaced steppe-grass-covered mounds. My group drove to the north end of the village and then carefully counted the mounds to reach the one I thought might have been the home of my great-great-grandparents.

Inexact, I know. Even one extra out-building in one family's farmyard could have thrown our count off. And there was really no way to know if I was in the right spot. But as I posed for a photo on that grass-covered mound, then searched the area for a shard of the original red tile roof, I felt as though I'd made a tiny connection with my family's past.

Making your travel plans

If you've decided that ease of planning is most important to you and you have a minimum number of specific places you want to visit, you'll probably opt for a package tour. Try local travel agencies, search the internet, and ask friends and family members for package recommendations that will best meet your needs.

If you've decided to travel independently, you have some decisions to make about travel arrangements and what you want to see in your ancestral town. We'll cover that later in this chapter.

If you've decided to use a specialty travel group, you'll need to locate the best one for your location. Read on!

Finding a specialty travel group

A specialty or heritage tour group is your best bet if you want the convenience of someone else organizing your trip but want to be sure to visit your specific ancestral town. The most reliable way to find a specialty tour group that will meet your needs is to network with other genealogists specific to your area of interest, perhaps through joining a genealogy organization, websites, or Facebook groups and pages.

My family background is very specific—I'm a Black Sea German. My ancestors were ethnically German, but from the late 1700s to the early 1800s, they all immigrated to villages in Imperial Russia, in a region near the Black Sea that is now Ukraine and Moldova. In addition to helping me with my research, joining a Germans from Russia genealogy organization also made me aware of organized trips to Ukraine with tour operators who had excellent local contacts with people in my ancestral towns.

In addition to finding the tour organization I used for one trip to Ukraine, I connected with other like-minded people interested in this type of travel. So when I did go on that trip, I went with 12 colleagues rather than 12 strangers. We may or may not have been compatible if we were randomly thrown together simply through common travel schedules.

For another trip to Ukraine, I traveled on a semi-independently planned trip with three friends I met in this genealogy organization. With this small group, we could set our own travel plans and even change them midway through the trip when we wanted more time somewhere.

If you're looking for a specialty tour group, check out my website www.carolynschott.com/ancestry-travel for my up-to-date list on travel resources for planning your trip. If you don't find an option there, a few other suggestions are:

- Subscribe to publications that relate to your family's background. These specialty tour agencies usually advertise there.
- Search the internet using key words such as specialty travel genealogy, heritage travel, genealogy travel, family history travel, genealogy vacation, or ancestral travel.

Of course, you'll want to do your due diligence and check out the travel firm's credentials and reputation. You may ask to speak with past travelers before sending in a deposit.

Making your own travel arrangements

If you're willing to take on responsibility for the trip planning, traveling independently of a tour group gives you great flexibility. It gives you the most control over your schedule and the places you visit. It often allows you to make more personal connections with people in the place you're visiting, rather than just with the other people in your group. The appendix of this book has a number of travel resource suggestions to help you with your travel planning.

One of my best experiences was traveling to Gyönk, Hungary, ancestral home of my Klein family. I spent the day with Janos, the town mayor (who also ran the local German heritage museum), and was invited to lunch with his wife and him. Not only did I get a tour of the town and cemetery, but I also got a glimpse into the daily lives of the people living in Gyönk today through my conversations with Janos, his wife, and the local pastor.

Although the visit started off with some formality—the town mayor escorting a visiting American—that formality was soon discarded when Janos got into my rental car and discovered how badly I drove a stick shift. (This was the only rental option in Budapest, and my only experience driving a stick shift before this trip was a half hour in a Seattle parking lot as a friend tried to show me the basics.)

Hesitantly at first, Janos began to coach me on when to shift, which opened the door to a conversation about driving customs in Hungary versus the U.S. A little laughter (first mine, then he joined in) at my ineptness shifted the tone of our conversation from formal tour to conversational. At the end of the day, Janos insisted I return to his home and share a Hungarian aperitif with his wife and him before driving back to Budapest.

While the arrangements for this trip were a bit complicated to figure out on my own, it became a much richer and more personal visit than I could have experienced with any tour group. As I left Gyönk, I waved good-bye with genuine regret, having spent time with some great people I never would have met, or laughed with, or shared a meal with, otherwise.

Appointments

If you want to visit archives or libraries to do research, you'll definitely want to find out the hours they're open, their policies about visitors, and if an appointment is necessary to use their materials, microfilm readers, or computers.

Even if you're going to an ancestral town just to look around and don't have a specific agenda, making contact in advance with someone local can often enhance your visit. Churches, which most people want to see, are often locked during the week. If you want to visit a specific home or meet new relatives, advance contact is even more important. Even the most hospitable people may find it disconcerting to have a stranger show up on their doorstep saying, "Hi, we're related," or "Hi, my family used to live in your house." In small towns, contact the local town hall, the mayor, a local museum, or the church pastor.

Opening communication before you arrive is a great way to make some personal connections. I first contacted Marie-Luise because the pastor in one of my ancestral towns recommended her due to her interest in local history. We'd been in contact by email, and I paid her to do some research for me. So when I was traveling to Germany, I definitely wanted to meet her.

In person, we really hit it off. She showed me around several villages in the area, explaining the complex history of how these different villages had belonged to different German princes. I got to see the inside of the church in my village and meet the pastor's wife. We visited a little-known local museum and met with an elderly woman who knew a lot of local history. We even sat in Marie-Luise's living room, looking through a 16th-century tax book that the local archive had entrusted to her.

On my next visit, I stayed with Marie-Luise rather than in a hotel, and she looked positively insulted when I tried to pay her for some additional research she'd done for me. "We are friends now; I will not charge you!"

In a way, there wasn't much to see in this ancestral town—no cemeteries or houses that I knew to be connected to my family. But with Marie-Luise as my guide, I got a great overview of the history of the area and met some interesting people I would never have met by going to a museum or simply walking through a cemetery. And I made a friend!

Of course, sometimes an unplanned visit does work. An older woman and her two granddaughters showed up at my house in Seattle one Saturday. The woman had lived in my house when she was a child, the family (who all lived elsewhere now) happened to be in Seattle visiting friends, and she wanted her young granddaughters to see the house where she'd grown up.

I decided she didn't look like an ax murderer, so I invited her in. She gave me a tour of my own home, describing the changes that had been made over the years. She and her sister had shared what was now my bedroom, and she drew a line in the air to show where they'd had a strip of tape to stake out their own halves of the room.

I could tell she enjoyed seeing her old home again; her

granddaughters got to see a bit of their family's history, and I learned some things about my own home I'd never known.

Language and translators

If you're traveling outside of the U.S. as a tourist, you can usually get along fine knowing English and being willing to try a little impromptu sign language. English has become a world language and most countries' tourist facilities (hotels, transportation companies) are staffed with at least some English speakers. Even if you get into a momentary situation where no one around you speaks English, you can generally point or pantomime what you need.

But if you travel outside of tourist areas as you visit small ancestral towns or archives, the chance of finding English speakers goes down rapidly. If you want to know specifics about a village's history or about using a microfilm reader, pantomiming is unlikely to work well. In that case, if you don't speak the local language yourself, you may want to find out how to hire a translator or ask in advance if someone is available who speaks English.

If you don't speak the language and don't have a translator, consider using Google Translate (if you have internet access) or a translation app on your phone (most convenient if it doesn't rely on the internet). Another great translation tool is the book *Point it: Traveller's Language Kit*, which is a picture dictionary that allows you to communicate by pointing at pictures.

On a recent trip to ancestral towns in Poland, I followed a suggestion from my cousin Justin, who has also done a lot of travel to ancestral places. I created a page of simple sentences, then used Google Translate to create Polish versions. (My name is Carolyn. My German ancestors lived in this village about 1800. Is there an old German cemetery?) It worked wonderfully in one village, and the people I talked to really engaged in reading it and pointing me in the direction of the cemetery. (It worked less well in the other village, but I think I just caught people in the middle of their work day, and they didn't have time to deal with a random American wandering around their town.)

Another option would be to create questions along with multiple choice answers for them to point at. The question "Who lived in this house before you?" might have multiple choice answers like: (a) my parents and grandparents; (b) I bought it from someone I know; (c) I bought it from a stranger; (d) I don't know. This method can provide more information than if they just launch into a long, detailed explanation in a language you don't understand.

I haven't found standard foreign language phrase books and apps to be very useful. These usually focus on tourist-related words and phrases, rather than those useful when visiting an ancestral town. Knowing how to say "Where can I buy a ticket?" is less useful than "My ancestors lived here in the 18th century, and I would like to see the inside of your house."

Do Your Genealogy Ahead of Time

If your main goal is to visit your ancestral town (versus a research-focused trip), you'll definitely want to do your genealogy ahead of time rather than expect that you will find out information in your town. Most church records no longer reside in the original towns and are now in church archives, so you'll be disappointed if you have high expectations for unlocking new clues. And although you may meet distant cousins with all the genealogical answers you've been seeking, you can't count on that happening.

When I went to Ober-Gleen, Germany, I knew it had been the birthplace of my five-times great-grandfather Michael Schott. Although he moved away from the village, he left behind his sister Anna Elisabetha whose married surname was Jacobi. When I asked around, it turned out that there was a large Jacobi family still in the village. Unfortunately, they knew little about their genealogy back to the 1600s, and I hadn't researched Anna Elisabetha's descendants. I probably had distant cousins that I could have met if I'd done my homework.

Come prepared

You'll want to have family history information with you when you meet a potential distant cousin or want to verify that the gravestone you're looking at is really your ancestor. It's usually best if this isn't Wi-Fi dependent, so paper or a phone app is best for this.

It's also useful to bring along any village maps or historic photos you might have of the village to show to locals so they can help you locate important buildings (your ancestor's home or the site of a church or town hall that may have been torn down or repurposed).

And then there are the basic things, such as being sure to have extra batteries for your camera or a notepad to write down information. These things can seem small but can lead to huge disappointment if you don't have the right tools at the moment when you finally find that gravestone or talk to your grandmother's former next-door neighbor who knows more about your family than your own family does.

Doing research during your travels

If you want to do genealogical research in your family's ancestral town (or a nearby library or archive), you'll definitely want to do some preplanning. You'll want to make some contacts in the place where you're going before you leave on your trip, and you'll want to be sure to come prepared with your specific genealogy data. Some archives or libraries require an appointment to use microfilm readers or to ensure that someone who can help you is there.

When planning a research trip to Germany, I discovered the Hessen state archive had an online catalog. Not only did this help me develop a list in advance of the documents that I wanted to review at the archive, but I discovered these documents were in the Wiesbaden branch archive rather than the (more obvious) Darmstadt main archive. This was critical to my trip planning; otherwise, I would have ended up in the wrong city to do my research. This also helped me make the best use of my time at the archive. I could focus on looking at the documents rather than spending time figuring out which ones were likely to help me. Therefore, doing a little advance planning made this archive visit much more productive than if I'd just shown up on the doorstep.

If you plan to do research while on your trip, it's good to have an idea of what you're looking for and to bring along whatever information you need from your own records at home.

A Few Last Tips

Here are a few miscellaneous tips for your ancestral town travels that I've learned over the years:

- Ask anyone and everyone for help. Sometimes the grumpy old men (or even the drunk old men!) and the little old ladies eyeing you suspiciously while sitting on a bench snapping peas in their garden can turn out to be your most helpful sources.
- Find the mayor or town hall or any other local administration to find out more about the history of the village. They may direct you to a museum or school or local history enthusiast.
- When you're in your ancestral town, don't be shy. Engage in conversations. It can be a delightful way to get to know the locals and maybe find out information about your family. I thoroughly enjoyed the debate in the town of Freudental (Myrne, Ukraine) about whether a specific house had previously belonged to Germans. We started talking with the owner of the house who had recently purchased it and wasn't sure. More neighbors joined in to offer their opinions, and the conversation moved out into the street and down to another neighbor's home. Someone suggested that yet another person would know, and the whole conversation group drifted down the street to find out his pronouncement. I'm not sure that we

ever decided, but it was great fun engaging the neighborhood in the lively debate.

- If you meet someone (or see something) with one of your family names, introduce yourself and ask questions. It could lead to some serendipitous new discoveries. Of course, that doesn't happen every time. I tried so hard to get a conversation going with a winemaker at a family winery in Osthofen. I love wine, and the family name was Müller, which was one of my family names from that village. I know Müller is a common name, but after all, my people were also from that village. Yet I couldn't get more than a grunt or "uh huh" from him. Oh well.

- Bring back a piece of your village. Of course, don't do anything illegal or bring back anything Customs would frown on when you're trying to re-enter your home country. But a stone or small amount of dirt or pressed flower can make your memory of the visit very tangible when you're back home.

- Be aware of places where your family traveled through, even if they didn't spend enough time there for you to consider it an ancestral town. That gives you the opportunity to plan a genealogy-related side trip if you happen to be nearby. While vacationing in London, my cousin took a day trip to Southampton, England, as his family had traveled to America on a ship that stopped there. The local library helped him find the newspaper announcement about the ship's arrival and departure times, giving him all sorts of interesting details about local weather and events. Although the stop in Southampton was not a major part of his family's story, it provided a few more details and a little color to the dry facts he'd previously known about their voyage to America.

- Sleep in your ancestral village if you can. My cousin Justin, who visited the village of Neudorf (Karmanova, Moldova) said, "I know it's not always easy, but I loved knowing that I had slept in Neudorf 70 years after the last Ehresmann had left. *Loved* it."

- As preparation for your travel to your ancestral town, or as a substitute while you're saving up for that dream trip, consider a virtual visit by zooming in on the town using Google Earth (www.google.com/earth) or finding photos of the town by going to maps.google.com, hovering over "Satellite" and clicking on photos.

Ending a happy day in Gräfenhausen

In Their Footsteps

A Village of Quiet Charm
(Original blog post: July 30, 2016)

My 1999 visit to Gräfenhausen (origin of my Billigmeier family) epitomizes what not to do when visiting an ancestral town. I showed up there one afternoon, completely unplanned. I stood on the street, looked around, didn't talk to anyone (didn't actually see anyone to talk to), took a photo of a building that looked important, stood in the cemetery (no Billigmeier graves), then left. I was probably there about 20 minutes in total.

Visiting last week was a completely different experience, thanks to the warmth and hospitality of the people of Gräfenhausen. The visit helped me fall in love with the quiet charm of this small village, tucked into a wooded valley north of Annweiler.

Herr Unger, a life-long resident, gave me a glimpse into the life and history of Gräfenhausen, his love for his home village shining through with every word. And fortunately, Herr Koelsch, who runs the Annweiler Heimatmuseum, assisted both with translation and by giving me additional background on the history of the area.

I was welcomed into that "important-looking" building (the town hall) that I'd taken a photo of 17 years ago and seated in the mayor's seat. (Although technically, Gräfenhausen is part of Annweiler and run by its mayor, the village does have its own community leader.) Herr Unger pulled out a bottle of local wine, and we sipped a lovely red as we talked over 500 years of history.

It's a small town, without jaw-dropping sights to see. Instead, I got a very personal glimpse of life there as Herr Unger pointed out the historic-looking homes of his parents, grandparents, and cousins. As he showed me the stables, garden, and smokehouse, his description painted a picture of a family growing up in small-town Germany after WWII.

Going back to my ancestors' time, I learned how this area had been occupied by the French in the late 1700s and how hard life had been in the early 1800s despite the end of the French occupation—no doubt the reason that free land in Ukraine was an attractive enough offer to entice my family to travel 1,400 miles east.

I learned that there was no Protestant church in the village at that time and imagined my ancestors walking a little over a mile each Sunday down the valley to the church in Queichhambach. I learned how methodical the farmers of Gräfenhausen were—wine grapes planted on one side of the valley and all other crops planted on the other side. I discovered that there was a book about the history of Gräfenhausen, and I was actually in the village long enough to purchase one (from the one store in town, which is only open from 6:00 a.m. to 11:00 a.m.).

My hosts in my Ferienwohnung (vacation apartment) in a local winery were warm and welcoming (and happened to be cousins of Herr Unger), curious about my centuries-old connection to their town. They got very engaged in helping me look for possible Billigmeier families (unfortunately, there were only a few in the online telephone directory and even those had a different spelling) hoping to help me find distant cousins.

My only regret was that the local Gasthof, a restaurant with a small beer garden, was closed due to the owner's illness. I'd had visions of drinking beer with the locals and getting to know a few more people, embracing daily life in the village if only for an evening.

Gräfenhausen sits at the end of the road, up against the wooded slopes of the surrounding hills. No one ends up in Gräfenhausen accidentally—it's not on the way to anywhere. It seems a remote location and is—most people living there work in the city of Landau, about 10 miles away. Gräfenhausen residents are often asked why they stay, why they don't move nearer work and the city. But the small community is a close-knit one, with families whose roots stretch back dozens, sometimes hundreds, of years. Its quiet charm is causing it to grow (lots of new construction happening) despite its remote location because people want to experience that quiet sense of community.

I finished my day sitting on the deck of my room, sipping a chilled local rosé, and listening to the shouts from a soccer match and postgame party at the community center. It made me wish that my connection to this community was a little closer than 200 years.

Chapter 7

Seeking Out Social History

Visiting the local museum in Osthofen, where my ancestors were linen weavers, I experimented with the loom on display.

Exploring Your Ancestors' Lives

Walking the streets where your ancestors once lived creates a special connection with the lives they experienced. I love strolling along, imagining my ancestors looking at the same buildings and streets as they rushed to the marketplace or to church.

But trying to picture it as it looked when my family lived there often leaves me wondering—what were their days really like? Did they get up and have coffee in their bathrobe like I do? (Did they even have bathrobes?) Did they ever look around the kitchen and wonder what to cook for dinner like I do? (Maybe, but they probably didn't have many choices.) What were their lives really like?

Sometimes my ancestors seem somewhat two-dimensional as I

only know names and dates. It's hard to think of them as real people, who caught colds and played with their children and were afraid of spiders. If you're lucky enough to have family letters (which I don't), those might give you a glimpse into their hopes and dreams and problems. But often there isn't enough detail to understand their daily lives.

I often wish for a time machine so I could take the ultimate ancestral town trip (visiting the place *and* time where they lived). But since that's not practical, my best advice is to get a peek into the social history of your family heritage by incorporating explorations of the food, customs, daily chores, and history of your ancestors as you visit your ancestral town or country.

What Did They Eat?

Many of my family's photos focus on family around a table or at picnics. Some of my fondest memories of childhood are the special dishes that Mom used to make. Sometimes even a smell can give me a flashback to family Thanksgivings at our house or Christmas dinner at my Aunt Edna's.

My favorite meals were the "dough" dishes—dumpling-like foods that my mother made because her mother made them because her mother made them. It was a welcoming homecoming when I found these dishes in Ukraine, where my German ancestors lived for 100 years before coming to the States. And it was a bit of a surprise when I traveled to Germany the first time and couldn't find the strudels or cabbage rolls or *käse knepfla* of my youth anywhere. My family favorites were apparently more deeply influenced by the generations in Ukraine than their German origins.

A visit to your ancestral homeland allows you to seek the local food culture, creating an interesting travel experience that deepens your understanding of your family roots. Don't just eat a croissant and feel you've celebrated your French heritage—explore!

Food explorations

Take a cooking class

One of my best travel experiences ever was a week-long cooking class in Greece. Although my ancestral background is not Greek, I claim Greece as my adopted country because I lived there for the good part of a year in my 30s, and fell in love with the people and culture. Learning to prepare foods from different regions, wandering the island to pick herbs to use in our cooking, attempting (sort of successfully) to milk a goat, and staring at an octopus in the sink ready to be cooked for lunch gave me a much deeper appreciation for Greek heritage.

Visit food-themed museums or drives

Exploring museums focused on foods important to your ancestral land can enrich your understanding of your ancestors' lives. When I was introducing my cousin's daughter to Germany (her first trip, my umpteenth trip), I focused initially on big-name sights, such as the Rhine River, Rothenburg ob der Tauber, and castles. But I'd mentioned my love of quirky museums to her and that I'd always regretted never visiting the Bread Museum. It was a thrilling moment for me when she said, "Why don't we go?" She's an adventurous cousin after my own heart (or tolerant of my travel quirks), because visiting a Bread Museum cannot possibly be high on every college student's list for a dream trip to Germany.

But I found it fascinating. The museum exhibits described different agricultural methods for growing wheat and displayed a map where I traced the route of my farming ancestors through the world—all wheat-growing regions. One exhibit showed how bread delivery and packaging evolved in Germany. It even talked about the significance of bread in several faith traditions. An impulsive stop became a fascinating peek into my ancestors' lives, growing wheat and living off the harvest (all those dumplings!).

Your ancestral region may have special routes identified, such as a cheese trail or wine trail or pasta trail, to guide you to local producers so you can sample their products. These drives or walks can be a great way to get off the beaten track and meet people who experience a modern version of your family heritage.

Stay in a farmhouse as an agritourist

Admittedly, not all of us have roots in farming communities. Still, most of our ancestors lived far closer to the land than we do today, so staying in a farmhouse and participating in the rhythm of daily life provides an opportunity to better understand how your ancestors fed themselves. In one such agritourist B and B that I visited in Greece, everything served was farm-to-table. They grew the grapes to make their wine and raised chickens for eggs and meat. They even used old, dried-up grapevines as fire material when smoking meats. Living off the land and being self-sufficient is how many of our ancestors survived. Experiencing that for yourself illustrates in a personal and dramatic way the differences between our ancestors' lives and our own.

Go to a grocery store

I love going to grocery stores in other countries. I remember grocery shopping when I lived in Greece and being confronted with a whole aisle full of canned calamari. Whole, chopped, I don't even know what all the variations were. And when I returned home to Seattle, I had a culture shock moment when confronted with a grocery aisle full of bottled water—sparkling, still, flavored. The differences in what items are considered important sustenance can be striking.

I suppose a modern grocery store isn't truly a glimpse into my ancestors' lives, but rather into the current-day culture of my ancestral place. But seeing how grocery stores use the real estate in their stores can be a fascinating insight into what's important in each culture and a reflection of the food traditions of that culture.

Try new foods

When traveling in places related to my family heritage, I'm tempted to look for the traditional favorites that my mom or aunts made—strudels, *knepfla*, *kuchen*. But I also challenge myself to try new things. Without that challenge, I would never have discovered *borshch* in Ukraine or sauerbraten in Germany (neither of which my family ever made). An unplanned stop at a winery in Schabo, Ukraine, was a very special experience because my travel buddies and I got to taste local wines in a Ukrainian wine-making village founded by Swiss Germans.

Of course, some surprises aren't so nice, like the time I tried *sülze* (headcheese) in Germany. If you've never experienced this, it's served in slices, sort of like meat loaf. But it's basically a gel, filled with meat parts from some (thankfully) unknown part of the pig. *Sülze* is a food tradition that I can't embrace. I am thankful my ancestors felt the same and didn't carry this tradition from Germany to Ukraine to the U.S.

What Were Their Days Like?

As I pop dishes into the dishwasher or visit the dentist for a tooth-saving crown, I often think, "I'm so glad that I live in a time with modern medicine and modern conveniences. How did my ancestors survive?" But I've realized that by focusing on the absence of things I take for granted, I've thought very little about what was actually present in my ancestors' lives.

What did they do for fun? What were their stores and schools like? How did young men meet young women? What did they have for breakfast?

Exploring their daily lives

Visit a living history museum

I find living history museums a fascinating glimpse into another time. Talking with people who are dressed in period clothing and using historical kitchenware to make meals or using a last to shape shoes by hand provides a glimpse into a life far removed from my own 21st century existence. When you see how hot and dirty it was in a blacksmith's shop or see a loaf of bread come out of the oven flecked with ash from the wood burning in the oven, Great-Grandma Sonja and Great-Grandpa Lars become more than just names in a family tree defined only by dates in a church register.

I remember visiting Plimouth Plantation in Massachusetts as a child on a family vacation and having one of the living history actors drop out of character to admit to my mom that he was really glad he was getting off duty in a couple of hours so he could go home and have a normal meal. "What the Pilgrims had to eat was awful," he confessed.

Visit local heritage museums

Even if there's not a living history component that includes demonstrations of cooking or farm work, you can learn a lot about your heritage at local museums. Visiting village museums in Gyönk, Hungary, and Friedenstal (now Myrnopillya), Ukraine, which were re-creations of old German farms there, gave me a better understanding of the size of my ancestors' homes, who slept where, how far they had to go to their fields each day, and how the household chores, like drawing water from the well and cooking, were done.

Attend a local folk festival

Local festivals can be a fun immersion into experiencing your ancestors' lives. Of course, your timing has to be just right so you're in your ancestral region when a festival is taking place. But it's worth doing some research to find local festivals near your travel dates and planning around them.

In Germany, cousins took me to the local *Schlachtfest*—aka a "butcher-the-pig" festival. I actually saw no pigs butchered (as that would be embracing my ancestors' lives a bit more than this city girl could handle). But we ate traditional foods (sausage, made from the unfortunate pig), saw demonstrations of old-time skills and crafts, walked through traditional farm homes and schools, and even played a traditional game (sort of like musical chairs, but in a sheep pen).

Seeing sauerkraut being made gave me insight into a family story that I'd never quite understood. First the cabbage is kneaded with a big stick in a barrel. Then a cover is placed over the cabbage and held down with a rock to ensure the cabbage would be submerged in the brine and ferment properly.

A distant cousin of mine once told me that when his branch of the family came to the States, his grandmother brought along her sauerkraut rock from Bessarabia, having heard there were no rocks in North Dakota. A lack of rocks in North Dakota is funny in and of itself (my dad's often-stated reason for not wanting to be a farmer was because he was tired of picking rocks out of the North Dakota fields). But I never understood how a rock played a part in making sauerkraut until I saw this demonstration. Poor grandma apparently pictured a life without sauerkraut after her emigration and thought it would be a grim life if she didn't take matters into her own hands.

How Were They Affected by the World Around Them?

In history class, we always learn the big-picture history—Paul Revere and the American Revolution, Abe Lincoln and the Civil War, the Gold Rush, Pearl Harbor and WWII. And it's true that many of these events did affect our ancestors, just like the Vietnam War or 9/11 or the global recession of 2008 affected our own lives.

But for most people, local everyday events have a much greater impact than the grand, sweeping issues of the day. I never learned about the building of the Grand Coulee Dam in history class. But if it weren't for the Grand Coulee Dam, I probably wouldn't have grown up in Seattle, and my life would have been much different. (The opportunity for good jobs working on the dam brought my Great-Aunt

Viola and her husband to Washington . . . and Viola brought my mom to Washington . . . which is what caused my dad to come to Washington.)

Learning about local historical events can help you better understand the environment that influenced the decisions your ancestors made about their lives and work and where to live.

Exploring their history

Visit local museums

Local museums are the best way to find out the detailed bits of history that might have affected your ancestors. You may discover your village was a haven for French Huguenots fleeing persecution, or the center of a battle between local nobles, or that it experienced a flood in 1872 that devastated crops and caused people to flee. None of these things would be reported in standard history books but may have been an important turning point in your family's story.

When I traveled to my ancestral town of Ober-Gleen, I visited the local museum in nearby Kirtorf. I learned that an important industry in the area was a process that converted tree pitch to wagon-wheel lubricant (who knew?). As the aggressive tree harvests deforested the area, the industry went into a decline, as did the towns in the surrounding area. This may be one of the reasons my ancestor Michael Schott left to settle in the village of Osthofen near the Rhine River, which was rebuilding after the War of the League of Augsburg (1688-1697), which is sometimes called the War of the Palatine Succession. Building up something new probably sounded like a more promising future than a declining town. This is an obscure bit of history that I would never have learned without visiting this museum.

Look for museums that reflect your family's religious or occupational heritage

For example, if your ancestry is French Huguenot (French Protestants who were persecuted by the Catholics and fled France), a visit to your ancestral town in France will be interesting but may not reveal their life experiences as vividly as visiting the Huguenot Museum in Rochester, England, to gain a deeper understanding of the persecution your ancestors endured.

If your family lived in an area that focused on a specific industry (winemaking, olive oil, car manufacture), visit a museum related to your ancestors' livelihood. You'll learn more about your ancestors' work and may even find information to further your research. My friend Jackie received some valuable clues in her genealogy search from the Ford Motor Company museum and archive because her grandmother's cousin worked at Ford in the 1940s.

Find books about the local area

Local books will have details about the history of your ancestral area that you're unlikely to find elsewhere. When you visit that local museum, ask if they have books for sale or know of some available elsewhere in the vicinity. I found a great book on my village of Gräfenhausen in the small local grocery store. You can also check at the town hall or a library for local history books.

Sometimes you have to do a little sleuthing. I found the history book on my ancestral town in North Dakota for sale at the bank—where I would never have looked without being directed there. If your ancestral town has a Facebook page or website or any other presence on social media, try to connect with people there to get suggestions.

Don't balk just because the book is in a language you don't understand. Google Translate does an adequate job of translating text so you can get a general idea of what was written. This gives you the option to decide if there are sections that need professional translation to help you understand in detail.

Try a walking tour

Your family may have farmed olives in a remote Tuscan village, which is unlikely to have organized tourist activities. But you can still learn a lot by finding the nearest city (like, say, Siena) and joining a walking tour to learn about the history of the city and the area. I tend to like walking tours more than bus tours because the tour guide focuses on telling stories rather than just quickly pointing out famous sights as you drive past them. "Look, there's an important church on the right. And an important statue on the left." Those won't help you learn about your family, but the stories and history will.

A fresh batch of strudels on my stove

In Their Footsteps

Cooking in the Footsteps of My Ancestors
(Original blog post: November 16, 2015)

My mother was always blunt, or "direct" if you want to be polite. I learned to live with comments like, "Well, *that* hairstyle doesn't look good on you" or "You just have no sense of style" (when I preferred my own tailored look to her more flamboyant, sequin-bedecked clothing suggestions).

So it didn't really surprise me when she looked at her plate one Christmas Day and said, "These aren't right."

She was looking at the strudels I'd prepared, based on her own recipe. Little pockets of fluffy, dumpling-like goodness—tossed in the air until they're tissue-paper thin, rolled up and steamed over potatoes, and then served with gravy, sauerkraut, and North Dakota sausage. A delectable treat for anyone who grew up in a Black Sea German home. They were my favorite of all the German dishes my mom cooked when I was growing up. I'd spent years learning to make them myself, including coaching from my mom, my dad's cousin (for effective dough-stretching techniques), and my Aunt Idella.

"What's not right?"

"These. They're sort of hard."

Well, they tasted the same as always to me. When I pointed out that this hadn't prevented either of us from eating a plateful (I could be direct too), the conversation ended. Until the next day.

The phone rang, and when I answered it, the voice on the other end said, "Baking powder."

It took me a moment to realize this wasn't the typical approach of a telemarketer and that it was my mother's voice.

"How old is your baking powder? That's it. That's why they weren't right."

She obviously had been stewing on this all night. But I confess, I was a little annoyed with the "not right strudel" conversation, so I rolled my eyes, promised to check, and hung up. Later that morning, when I got around to making good on my promise, I discovered that my baking powder was past its expiration date—by seven years. Woops.

Fast forward to yesterday. It was a cold, rainy weekend in Seattle, and strudels seemed like the perfect antidote. Another important factor was that I planned to be home all day. The strudel recipe calls for the dough to rest a lot, so you have to be nearby to tend it.

I've learned to check my baking powder these days, and sure enough, mine was expired. But only by a month, and I didn't want to run to the grocery store. I decided it was still fine.

But it wasn't. My strudels did not live up to my mother's, aunts', or grandmothers' cooking. Probably not my great-grandmothers' either, but I never had a chance to try their strudels for myself.

Baking powder seems to be my Achilles heel of strudels. I can just sense the disappointment of centuries of Black Sea German ancestresses. I'm sure they whipped up a pot of strudels for the family dinner, flipping the dough up in the air while doing laundry with the other hand and tending small children underfoot.

They created doughy goodness in their primitive kitchens—no

running water, wood-fired stoves, a cellar across the yard providing the only refrigeration. By contrast, my kitchen is 21st-century elegance—granite tile, gas range, stainless steel appliances, and lots of doodads that peel, core, and chop. And yet, I was foiled by baking powder.

I've often visited my ancestral towns to walk in the footsteps of my ancestors. But I still struggle to cook in the footsteps of my ancestors. Sigh. Off to the store for more baking powder.

Chapter 8

The Trip of a Lifetime

A moment of silliness in the vineyard outside of Osthofen

Planning and Chance Create Memorable Trips

When things go right, your visit to your ancestral town lets you experience a little bit of the life your ancestors experienced. For me, the most memorable trips are those where I make personal connections, so the trip becomes more about the people rather than just the places.

Traditions live on

On my first trip to Ukraine, I visited Hoffnungstal, the village where my grandfather was born. I knew the village had been destroyed, so I wouldn't be able to see much.

Still, I walked on the hill where the cemetery had been. Though all the stones were gone, I knew that several generations of my family lay somewhere beneath my feet. I looked down into the valley that had once held a thriving village of several thousand people and imagined I was seeing it as my great-great-grandparents had when they first arrived there. I walked on the faint track worn through the steppe grasses and tried to see the street as it had been in my grandfather's time— wide and bordered with neatly whitewashed stone walls.

Later that evening, my traveling companions and I were staying at the home of Micha and Mascha, a Ukrainian couple who lived in a village a couple of miles away from Hoffnungstal. Mascha and her sister had made strudels for us, just like my mother had made. We didn't have a common language and had to rely on Serge, our guide, to translate for us. Despite this, the warmth of laughing and toasting together, and eating the foods I'd grown up with, gave me a sense of connection. Though my grandfather's village was gone, the traditions of food, hospitality, and gathering around a table in laughter remained unchanged.

From strangers to colleagues to neighbors

Bob, one of my genealogy colleagues, visited his ancestral town in Ukraine and the house where his grandfather had lived. As he got to know the family living there, a single woman supporting her daughter and her mother, he realized how difficult it was to support a family in the Ukrainian economy. With the unemployment rate at 70 percent in the nearby city of Mykolaiv, Valya had been unable to find a job. Her mother, Olga, had previously worked on one of the collective farms but did not receive a pension.

Bob looked for a way he could help this family that was more caring than simply handing them money and then flying back to the U.S. and forgetting them.

It took a few years of thought and planning, but Bob eventually started a specialized tour service for those of Black Sea German background to visit their ancestral towns in Ukraine. Valya became the tour organizer and guide; then later her daughter, Karolina, took over the business. As chance would have it, the tour business became the setting for romance. Valya married a man on one of the tours and moved to the same state where Bob and his family live.

Bob's visit to his ancestral town led to a long-term friendship between Bob and Valya's families, the business helped provide financial stability for Valya's family in Ukraine for many years, and the two families now live less than an hour apart in South Dakota. Talk about an impact he won't forget!

A sense of connection

Visiting my parents' hometowns in North Dakota has led to some important personal connections for me.

When I visited my mom's hometown of Lehr for its 100th anniversary celebration, I met my stepcousin Lynette. I suppose we'd met when we were kids, but she was one of the "big" kids, seven years older than me, and so we'd never known each other well. When Lynette's aunt was going to throw out a box of old stuff from her attic, Lynette looked at it and recognized the photos and documents were from my family. Knowing of my interest in genealogy, she decided to take it herself to give to me rather than let her aunt throw it away.

Without her intervention, my grandmother and mother's baptismal certificates, plus a number of family photos, would have been thrown in the trash. I was so thankful to have made that connection and gotten to know Lynette.

I also feel a real sense of connection when visiting my dad's hometown of Kulm. When I was a child, we went there almost every year on vacation, so visiting Kulm was not a particularly new or long-awaited experience for me. But a visit as an adult reminded me of my connection to this small town.

My cousin, who lives there, and I were walking down the street. My cousin stopped to talk with a couple of men, introduced me as his cousin, and added, "This is Harry's daughter." The men's nods and murmurs of assent showed they understood clearly where I fit in the family.

Although my dad had grown up in this town in the 1920s and '30s, he'd moved to Seattle almost 60 years before. We'd only visited a few days each summer after that, then my dad died about 30 years ago. Yet these men clearly knew who my dad was, how he fit into the family, and therefore how I fit.

I grew up in Seattle where a lot of people don't know their own cousins, let alone the cousins of friends and neighbors. This small encounter made me feel part of the thread of life in this small town because of my family connections.

Learning your own personal history

The visit my cousin-in-law Meatra made to her father's hometown in Cambodia helped her better understand her father's personality and ambitions. Family history information has been impossible to find because most records were destroyed during the Pol Pot regime (1970s) or lost when her family had to flee the country. Some of her family members were killed during that time, and so even the oral history and family stories have been lost.

But visiting her father's hometown, meeting her aunts and uncles for the first time, visiting the school her father attended, and seeing the rural village and bamboo houses on stilts all gave her a greater insight into her father's determination to build a new life for his family.

Sometimes a Disaster, Sometimes an Adventure

Traveling can be unpredictable, even when you've been a careful planner. Most problems are simply annoying, although on occasion a problem may have more serious consequences (health, passport problems). But if you're going on a long-planned-for and hoped-for trip to an ancestral town, anything that interferes can be emotionally disappointing too.

There are common sense ways of protecting yourself from specific problems. Travel insurance can help cover the cost of nonrefundable tickets if you need to cancel your trip or a natural disaster causes major delays. Travel medical insurance can help cover you if a health issue occurs. Checking references or ratings for an unknown travel agent, airline, or hotel can give you peace of mind that it is legitimate.

But the best way to protect yourself from the most common types of travel mishaps, such as flight delays or weather problems, is simply to have the attitude that you'll make the best of whatever happens. As a bonus, making the best of any situation can lead you to unexpected, positive experiences.

Problems visiting your ancestral town

Beyond common travel issues, there are some problems unique to visiting ancestral towns. For example, you can get incorrect information and go to the wrong town. On my first attempt to locate my ancestral town in Germany, one of the genealogy reference books I used showed my family had come from Ludwigsburg, Baden-Württemberg. Given the excellent reputation of this book and lack of time before I left on my trip, I assumed the information was correct.

Ludwigsburg is a beautiful town of around 90,000 people, with a small, ornate castle in the middle of town. It's fairly well-known in Germany but not known to most American tourists. I had no specific information about my family living in this town, so I couldn't look for a church or a house to visit. It was a large enough town that even finding a cemetery was difficult. So I just walked through the downtown square looking around.

I enjoyed the town as a tourist but really didn't feel any sense of familiarity or attachment. In fact, I was frustrated because I arrived at lunchtime and couldn't find any restaurants other than the Wienerwald (fast food) and a lot of German cafés, which have only ice cream and coffee drinks. Even though I knew it was silly, I kept thinking, "The way my family eats, any town without restaurants can't be the home of my ancestors!"

Although my reasoning was shaky, my conclusion turned out to be correct. When I returned home and did more research, I found out my family wasn't from Ludwigsburg but rather from a town called Osthofen. (I suspect they received their emigration papers in Ludwigsburg, and that's what caused the mistake in the reference book, but I have no actual proof of this.)

It was disappointing that I hadn't seen my actual ancestral town. But I enjoyed visiting a place most American tourists don't see. I enjoyed visiting the castle. I tolerated eating at the Wienerwald, and the ice cream was pretty good too. And on a subsequent trip to Germany, I managed to get to Osthofen. Even though Ludwigsburg wasn't my ancestral town after all, rather than consider it a wasted trip, I chose to make the most of my visit as a tourist in an unfamiliar spot.

Extra preparation can prevent these types of disappointments. When I was in Ukraine, our guide had the town of Gnadental (Dolynivka in Ukrainian) on our list of villages to visit but not Gnadenfeld (Blahodatne), where my grandmother was born. Gnadental is a larger, older ethnic German village in this area. Gnadenfeld is a small village that was founded much later. Serge, our guide, had never had anyone ask to go to Gnadenfeld, so had assumed I was mistaken and I really meant Gnadental.

But this time I'd done my homework. I knew the correct village, knew where it was on the map, knew for sure it wasn't Gnadental, and was able to get us to make a course correction and visit the village where my family had actually come from.

Of course, even when you find the right village, the visit can sometimes be disappointing. When my friend Elli visited the village of Sangerowka (Novomykhailivka), Ukraine, where her mother had grown up, she expected the cemetery would still be standing and the village would still exist. Her cousin had visited 10 years before and had described all this to her.

Instead, she found the gravestones removed from the cemetery, plowed over to plant more crops. Only a couple of houses were still standing; most were small piles of rubble with the wind swirling clouds of dust between them. The effects of time and abandonment had taken their toll.

My friend Rich thought he was heading for a similar disappointment. He'd hoped to spend a night in the house where his father had grown up in Speier (Pishchanyi Brid in Ukrainian). Before his trip, his guide Karolina had tried to arrange this, but the current homeowner insisted she didn't want anything to do with Rich. (Perhaps fearful he would try to stake some claim to the house?) Fortunately, once Rich was there in person, he was able to convince Nellie that he was no threat. She relented and allowed Rich and his wife to at least walk through the home and take photos.

Sometimes a bad tour guide can mess up your plans. On my first visit to Freudental (Myrne), our guide took us to the middle of the village and announced, "This is Freudental. The cemetery is gone; the church is gone; the school they're using now wasn't the one used in German times." Then she looked at me expectantly, apparently assuming I would say, "Okay, let's go then."

But I wasn't satisfied with two minutes in the village where my great-great-grandparents had met and married and where my great-grandparents had been born. Fortunately, our driver, Peter, and I had become buddies (despite his lack of English and my lack of Ukrainian). I ignored the guide and showed Peter the map I had of the village, and he started asking people on the street what was there.

With Peter's help (and the guide's grudging translation), I got to see the cemetery (mostly gone except a few headstones), the site of the original church, and the ruins of one of the community buildings. Sometimes you have to take matters into your own hands and use whatever allies you can find to make sure you can see what you want.

Health and injuries

Of course, sometimes more serious problems come up, like accidents or health issues or volcanic eruptions that cause flight cancellations. (I'm not kidding about the volcanic eruption—I was flying out of Germany the day Iceland's Eyjafjallajökull volcano erupted. It made for a long travel day.) Such unexpected events could cause you to cancel or cut short a trip, missing the ancestral towns you'd hoped to visit. There's very little you can do at this point other than be philosophical and know you'll have to plan another trip. And hopefully you've done your trip preparations well enough that you have either the resources or insurance to cover yourself.

But some situations can be salvaged. Having the attitude you're going to make the best of whatever comes up can take you a long way toward making the situation work and minimizing the disappointment.

On my first trip to Ukraine to visit ancestral towns, I was already in Europe when the 9/11 terrorist attack occurred in 2001. My friends were supposed to fly from the U.S. on September 13, but all air traffic in and out of the U.S. had been stopped. While our travel plans were among the most minor casualties of that tragic day, it did turn our arrangements upside down. We needed to quickly decide whether we were going to continue the trip or not; and if we did, how to change our plans.

We decided to go ahead and scrambled to change our flight, guide, and hotel reservations. Many of our friends told us we were crazy to be traveling out of the country during that period of uncertainty after the attack.

But traveling outside the U.S. in the wake of this terrorist attack actually gave our trip more meaning. I'll never forget the elderly man in Kassel (Velykokomarivka), Ukraine. Although age had left him infirm, physically and sometimes mentally, I'll never forget him standing in his home in rural Ukraine—no running water, three generations living in a one-room house—with tears flowing down his cheeks as he talked about the victims in New York's World Trade Center.

On another trip to Ukraine to visit ancestral towns, I had an inconvenient and painful accident. I was in Bosnia prior to meeting up with my friends, and I broke my foot by stumbling over the two-inch-high threshold of my hotel door.

This could easily have ruined my trip. I was given a "walking cast" (actually a bit of plaster around my heel, wrapped with flimsy gauze) that was too fragile for me to tromp around cemeteries and muddy, rutted roads in rural Ukraine. I was in pain and in tears and ready to give up, change my ticket, and head home.

But my friends and I had planned this trip for a long time, so it was disappointing to give up on it. Once the painkillers kicked in, I came up with a desperate plan to save my trip. (See "In Your Footsteps" at the end of this chapter.) But I was on that plane to Ukraine as planned, despite my mishap.

My biggest challenge was visiting Hoffnungstal, a village that was very important to me. On my last visit, I'd discovered that the memorial stone, commemorating the existence of the village, had been vandalized. But one of my German cousins had told me a new one had been built, and I wanted to see it. Also, my genealogy mentor Dale, who helped me start my own research and who had planned to be on this trip with us, passed away several months before. His family had also come from this village, and we'd planned a short silent memorial to him.

Our guide, Karolina, had a map that showed a dotted-line outline of a village, indicating this was a ghost town because it had been destroyed. We drove along the rutted dirt track, with no signs of life—not even sheep—for miles. Karolina kept asking me, "Does this look familiar?" because she'd never been there before. Finally, I recognized the contour of the land dropping toward the valley.

Just as I was pointing to a group of trees on a hill that matched my memory, the road dipped downward, and the van came to a halt. An enormous mud puddle lay across the road, with no way to know how deep it was. The fields were too uneven on either side to drive around. Vova, our driver, just shook his head and said a few words to Karolina. Even without knowing Ukrainian, I knew he was saying we couldn't go any farther.

I looked up the hill. Not an especially long walk, but the track was rocky and uneven. I'd broken my foot less than a week earlier, and the only thing protecting it was the orthopedic boot. The boot wasn't particularly comfortable to walk in, so hiking up this trail seemed like a bad idea. Everyone in the van looked at me. I was the only one with an interest in this village, so it was up to me whether we stayed or left.

It seemed crazy to hike up that hill, but even crazier to come half-way around the world, be so close, and not actually make it to this spot I'd so wanted to see. I just said, "Let's go," as I crawled out of the van. Inna grabbed my arm to help me, and several of my friends hovered nearby as we slowly hiked up the track toward the cemetery.

I had to pass up walking through the ruins of the town (impossibly far away in the valley below)—at least for this trip. But I made it to the cemetery, saw the memorial, and we let feathers fly in the wind to honor our friend Dale.

Was I especially courageous? Or foolhardy? No, I was just determined to make the best of the situation, even with a broken foot. Experiencing an ancestral town is worth a little inconvenience and hardship.

Me and orthopedic boot visit the memorial to the German settlers of Hoffungstal (Nadezhdivka), Ukraine

In Their Footsteps

Neither Rain nor Sleet nor Broken Foot
(Original blog post: May 1, 2016)

Sometimes it's the little things in life that are the most dangerous. I survived petting a lion in Zambia and driving through crazed Athens traffic. But I was done in by my hotel door in Bosnia. In my own defense, it was an exceptionally high door threshold that you truly had to step over, sort of like I've seen on some ships. I guess I didn't step quite high enough . . . and was down for the count.

When a night's sleep and a couple of Advil didn't alleviate the pain—well, okay, when I almost collapsed in a heap on the bathroom floor trying to put weight on that foot getting out of the shower—I decided some actual medical attention might be a good idea.

As charmed as I was by Mostar, the historic district (aka a sea of cobblestones) didn't seem like a promising place for modern medicine, so I made a run for the border, back to Croatia, which seemed like my best bet for finding western-style health care. Returning to Croatia also had the advantage of allowing me to stick with my original itinerary—which meant I'd have a hotel bed to sleep in that night.

I had this unarticulated (and stupid) idea in my mind that if I didn't take any painkillers, it would mean the injury was not that serious. As a result, struggling up and down stairs with my suitcase to get from hotel to car, multiple hours of driving with my foot throbbing, a 90-plus-degree day, and a stop at a clinic where they told me that they couldn't help me, had about done me in.

The last straw was when my rental car wouldn't start. Piercing pain with every step, hot sun beating down on my head, I felt the tears gathering. I hovered on the brink of a meltdown.

Only the reminder that at the end of the meltdown I'd still be in the same predicament held back the tears. The rental car company wasn't answering the phone, and I couldn't walk to get help. Finally, I swallowed my pride and unwillingness to play the helpless female and asked a group of men chatting in front of the clinic for help.

I'm not sure they spoke English, but my incoherent and frazzled look communicated better than words. But when the man who helped me was able to start the car within about a minute, I couldn't decide if I should grateful for his help or irritated that I hadn't figured it out myself.

The empty hospital

A moving car (and its air conditioning) revived me enough to face the next ordeal—the hospital in Korcula. The eerie emptiness when I walked through the front door was reminiscent of the Saturday night midnight horror movies I'd watched at childhood slumber parties. It seemed a bad sign that a hospital could be so devoid of life. I started opening doors and peering down hallways, "Hello? Is anyone there?"

Persistent wandering led me to the emergency room and then the radiology department, also deserted until I ignored all hospital rules and started peering into one exam room after another—"Hello?"—until a radiologist appeared.

Post-x-ray, I joined what must have been the only human beings in the building—a group of elderly Croatians in a waiting room. I don't know if they were waiting for medical care or this was just where they met for afternoon coffee, but I ignored their energetic chatter (since I don't speak Croatian) until I heard a doctor's voice mention an "Amerikanska." All eyes turned to me. I guess I stood out a little.

Fortunately, the doctor spoke English. Unfortunately, he confirmed what I'd feared—the foot was broken. I was introduced to a Croatian cast—a bit of plaster on my heel wrapped in lots of gauze. He assured me it was a walking cast and that when the gauze started falling apart, I could come back and get it rewrapped. I did not find that comforting as I wasn't sure it would last through the parking lot to get back to my car.

Perseverance

Foot wrapped, I found myself stuck at an uninspiring all-inclusive tourist hotel with mediocre food, unable to walk without my "cast" falling apart. Not only would I miss my planned days of wandering the streets of old town Korcula, I had no idea whether my gauze-wrapped foot would hold up (or not) to the main part of my trip—tromping through ancestral villages in rural Ukraine, which would involve a lot of unpaved, dusty roads, goose-poop-filled yards, and overgrown cemeteries. Should I just cancel that part of the trip and fly home?

Suddenly, I had a flash of inspiration and sprang into action. The plan:

1. Figure out how to make an international call to Seattle (not the simple process it is these days).
2. Ask (in desperate tone) a Seattle friend to go to my house, barge in on my house sitter, and retrieve an orthopedic boot (previous foot injury) from my closet.
3. Have my friend ship the boot to Vienna using overnight delivery, which actually takes two days with the time difference.
4. Call the hotel in Vienna and beg them to accept the package, even though it will arrive before I'm checked in (which is against their policy).
5. Worry for two days about whether my plan will work.
6. Arrive at the hotel in Vienna (flying in from Croatia) two hours after boot's arrival.
7. Borrow desk scissors and snip off my Croatian cast (remember, it's mostly gauze) and insert foot into orthopedic boot.

8. Meet my friends for the flight to Odessa as planned. Next stop—rural Ukraine!

Genealogists are like the postal service—neither rain, nor sleet, nor a broken foot will keep us from tromping through cemeteries and ancestral towns.

Chapter 9

What's Next?

Singing with my hostess, Marina, in Kyiv, Ukraine

Further Exploring Your Family History

I hope this book has inspired you to take the next step on your journey, whether that is to take an adventure by visiting an ancestral town or dive more deeply into finding an elusive ancestor.

Sparking an interest

My first visit to my ancestral towns—my parents' hometowns—happened at about the age of nine months when my family made a road trip from Seattle to North Dakota. We repeated that trip almost every summer as I grew up.

The vast expanses of prairie that my parents experienced in their childhood; the magic of a small town and being able to walk out my aunt's back door, through her backyard, and be on Main Street; the rhythm of life based around the seasons and the three-times-per-day blare of the town's siren (noon, 6:00 p.m., and 10:00 p.m.) were so different from my own daily existence in Seattle that it opened up a whole new world for me. I'm sure it was these annual trips to my parents' hometowns that whet my appetite to see other places where my family had lived.

As I learned more about my family history, my goals for what I wanted to see both expanded and became more narrowly focused. I needed to get involved in genealogical research of my family to find out more details about who they were, where they'd lived, and what they'd experienced. I didn't do my research with a specific plan to visit my ancestral towns, mostly just wanting a better understanding of my heritage and where I'd come from.

When I started visiting ancestral towns, of course, I loved learning more about where my family had lived and getting a glimpse of their lives there. But I found that I enjoyed getting to know the local people I met, even if they weren't directly connected to my family history, just as much as thinking about my ancestors. The people I've gotten to know and the places I've visited in my ancestral town travels have come to hold a special place in my heart.

Taking it to the next level

Where do you go from here? With everything you've learned, you should be ready—to start your research, tear down some genealogy brick walls, take a DNA test, or plan your travel to places where your family has roots.

Connecting with your family's history and visiting the places where they once lived can help you get a deeper sense of who you are and where you come from. Your journey may not always lead exactly where you plan. You may encounter unexpected people or events along the way. Embracing those serendipitous experiences becomes a part of your journey, a part of the family history you are creating as you search.

Appendix

Tools and Travel Resources

Genealogical Standards of Proof

As you dig into archives and old records, you might have to evaluate if you've found enough information to be sure you have identified your ancestor and the right ancestral town. The Board for Certification of Genealogists has developed the Genealogical Proof Standard. Because we can't all find the perfect set of records to document our ancestors' lives, the purpose of this standard is to give guidelines on what is "good enough" in your research.

Even if you're not a professional genealogist (most of us aren't), these standards are useful to keep in mind for your own genealogy. They can help you decide when it's safe to conclude you have the right information or have pulled together enough information to reach an informed conclusion. If you've covered the following five elements, you have done your best to reach a solid conclusion.

1. Reasonably exhaustive search

This is a formal way of saying "leave no stone unturned." Have you been thorough in looking at—and searching for—a wide range of sources (church records, civil records, land records, census records, etc.)? Are your sources high quality? (That is, not just talking to Great-Aunt Mathilda or looking in a database of undocumented data.)

The goal is to ensure that you haven't missed an important source, leading to new evidence coming up later that disproves the conclusion you've made about your ancestor.

2. Complete and accurate citation of sources

It's crucial to use high-quality, reliable sources and to document those sources. This way, if you, or your great-grandchildren after you, ever want to go back and verify what you've found, any of you can follow the same trail and come to the same conclusion. This is basic in science—an experiment should be repeatable by someone other than the original scientist to be credible. If another genealogist can follow your trail, you've probably come to the right conclusion.

3. Analysis and correlation of the collected information

Almost all of us have been thrilled at some time by reading a murder mystery—seeing the clues unfold and then shaking our heads as we think "I would never have guessed it was him!" when the detective cleverly puts all the clues together and determines the murderer.

This is where you look at all the information you've gathered, look at the sources you have and how reliable they are, and draw your conclusions about your ancestor based on the evidence you've uncovered. It's important that all your evidence supports your conclusions and that you're not ignoring any facts simply because they don't seem to fit your interpretation. If that's the case, there may be an even more interesting answer. You'll just have to keep digging to find it.

4. Resolution of conflicting evidence

Often, we have conflicting evidence about where and when an ancestor was born, married, died, or lived. One ancestor of mine was born in 1816 in the village of Neudorf, according to multiple reliable sources, mostly church records. Yet a census of Neudorf taken in 1816 did not show the family in that village. Conflicting data, both from reliable sources.

For years, I had a question mark by this piece of data. I couldn't resolve the conflict because all of my sources were equally reliable. Another researcher finally helped me out; he'd found a copy of an addendum census in another archive that showed my family and one or two others arrived in the village in the fall of 1816, after the original census was taken in the spring. Finally, my conflicting data was resolved with a reasonable explanation, and I deleted the question mark.

5. Soundly reasoned, coherently written conclusion

Basically, this is your final conclusion, based on all the data you've gathered and after resolving any conflicts. As a hobby genealogist, it may seem like overkill to write out your conclusion. But I've found it to be immensely helpful to document in the notes section of my genealogy software the evidence I used to reach the conclusion I did. That helps me retrace my steps (with thousands of ancestors in my genealogy database, I can't always remember why I decided to believe one date or location over another). I also have my family tree online for others to access, so it will help them better understand the data as they incorporate it into their own family tree.

Interview Guide

When interviewing a family member about family history, your basic strategy is to get them talking and remembering. It's often best to start off with open-ended questions such as "Tell me about your parents and what you remember about them," which (hopefully) will open a floodgate of anecdotes and information.

But if the person you're interviewing is a bit more reticent or gives you brief answers that don't provide much information, it can be helpful to have some prepared questions to draw them out.

Below is a list of more than 100 questions to help prompt your conversation. I wouldn't recommend showing your interviewee the long list—they might be terrified! This list is just a tool. Pick and choose the questions most likely to get your interviewee to open up.

At the end of your interview, I suggest asking "Is there anything I haven't asked about that you'd like to talk about?" I've found the new information that may pop out may be really amazing.

I also would suggest recording your interview to make it feel more like a conversation than an interview in which you're taking detailed notes, which can make the person being interviewed feel self-conscious.

Basic family information

Personal information

1. What is your full name? Why did your parents select this name for you? Did you have a nickname?
2. When and where were you born?
3. How did your family come to live there?
4. What do you know about your family surname?
5. Is there a naming tradition in your family, such as always giving the firstborn son the name of his paternal grandfather?
6. What is the full name of your present spouse?

7. When, where, and how did you first meet your present spouse?
8. How long did you know him/her before you got married? What did you do on dates?
9. What was it like when you proposed (or were proposed to)? Where and when did it happen? How did you feel?
10. Where and when did you get married? (Include date, place, church, etc.)
11. Were you married more than once? If so, answer the previous questions about each spouse.
12. When and where did your spouse die?
13. How many children did you have all together?
14. What were their names, birth dates, and birthplaces?
15. Why did you give them the names that you did?
16. Do you remember any advice or comments from your parents or grandparents that had a big impact on how you lived your life?
17. What were the hardest choices you ever had to make?
18. What is the most stressful experience you ever lived through?
19. What is the single most memorable moment of your life?
20. Is there anything you have always wanted to do but haven't?
21. Were you ever mentioned in a newspaper?
22. Where was your first home?
23. In what other homes/places have you lived?
24. What was your profession, and how did you choose it?
25. What was your first job, and what other jobs have you had?
26. Did you serve in the military, when and where did you serve, and what were your duties? Rank?
27. Were you ever injured in the line of duty?
28. What was your religion growing up? What church, if any, did you attend? If that's different from your current religious practice, why did you change?
29. What was the religion of your parents and your grandparents?

Parents, grandparents, and other extended family information

30. Who were your parents? Please give full names.
31. Where were they born, and where did they grow up?
32. When and where did your parents die? What do you remember about it?
33. How did they die? Where were they hospitalized and buried?
34. What are the full names of your brothers and sisters?
35. Could you tell me a story or any memory of your brothers and sisters?
36. Where did your spouse's parents live?
37. What do you remember about the death of your spouse's parents?
38. Who were your grandparents? Please give full names.
39. Where were they born, and where did they grow up?
40. Were there other family members living in the same area when you grew up? Who?
41. Who was the oldest relative you remember as a child? What do you remember about them?
42. What stories have come down to you about your parents? Grandparents? More distant ancestors?
43. Are there any stories about famous or infamous relatives in your family?
44. Are there any physical characteristics that run in your family?
45. Do you remember hearing your grandparents describe their lives? What did they say?
46. Do you remember your great-grandparents?
47. Do you have any relatives who live in foreign countries?
48. Do you know which of your ancestors immigrated to America? Do you know where they came from? Have you heard any stories about how they traveled to America?
49. Do you have any family photos I can look at and make a copy of?

50. Has anyone else in the family ever gathered genealogy information? Who?

Family events and daily life

Questions about daily activities can help you better understand your relatives' lives and the events that most influenced them.

Home

1. What was the house (apartment, farm, etc.) like where you grew up? How many rooms? Bathrooms? Did it have electricity? Indoor plumbing? Telephones? Computers?
2. Were there any special items in the house that you remember?
3. What are your earliest memories of your home?

Personal memories

4. Tell me about your earliest childhood memory.
5. Of all the things you learned from your parents, which do you feel was the most valuable?
6. Tell me about yourself as a young person. What were you like?
7. What accomplishments are you proudest of?
8. What is the one thing you most want people to remember about you?
9. Do you remember having a favorite nursery rhyme or bedtime story? What was it?
10. What were your favorite toys or games, and what were they like?
11. What kinds of books did you like to read?
12. How old were you when you started dating?
13. Do you remember your first date? Could you tell me something about it?
14. Name a good friend you have known the longest. How many years have you been friends?
15. What musical instruments have you learned to play?

16. What are your hobbies, or what do you like to do when you're not working?
17. What organizations or groups have you belonged to?
18. Have you ever won any special awards or prizes as an adult? As a child? What were they for?
19. What was the favorite place you ever visited, and what was it like?
20. As a child, what did you want to be when you grew up?
21. What was your favorite job and why?
22. How long did you have to work each day at your job?
23. Did you have any of the childhood diseases?
24. Do you have any health problems that are hereditary?
25. Have you ever been the victim of a crime?
26. Have you ever been in a serious accident?
27. Has anyone ever saved your life?
28. Have you ever saved someone else's life?
29. How do you feel about the choices you made in school, career, spouse?
30. How did you find out you were going to be a parent for the first time, and how did you feel about it?
31. How did you first hear that you were a grandparent, and how did you feel about it?
32. What advice do you have for your children and grandchildren about being a parent?
33. What advice would you give/did you give to your child or grandchild on his/her wedding day?

Family memories

34. What did your family enjoy doing together?
35. Did you have family chores? What were they? Which was your least favorite?
36. Did you have any pets? If so, what kind and what were their names?

37. Describe a typical family dinner. Did you all eat together as a family? Who did the cooking? What were your favorite foods?

38. How were holidays (birthdays, Christmas, etc.) celebrated in your family? Did your family have special traditions?

39. Have any recipes been passed down to you from family members?

40. Describe the personalities of your family members.

41. Are there any special heirlooms, photos, Bibles, or other memorabilia that have been passed down in your family?

42. Do you remember anything your children did when they were small that really amazed you?

43. How did you feel when the first of your children went to school for the first time?

44. If you had to do it all over again, would you change the way you raised your family?

School

45. What was school like for you as a child? Where did you attend grade school? High school? College?

46. What were your best and worst subjects and why?

47. Who was your favorite teacher, and why was he/she special?

48. Tell me about any school activities and sports you participated in. Did you ever win any awards?

49. Who were your friends when you were growing up?

50. How do your fellow classmates from school remember you best?

51. Did you and your friends have a special hangout where you liked to spend time?

Culture and society

Questions about culture, society, and daily activities can help you better understand the world in which your family member grew up.

1. What were your favorite songs and music in your youth?

2. Do you remember any fads from your youth? Popular hair-styles? Clothes?

3. What world events had the most impact on you while you were growing up? Did any of them personally affect your family?

4. How is the world today different from what it was like when you were a child?

5. Do you remember your family discussing world events and politics?

6. What wars have been fought during your lifetime?

7. What were you doing when you heard the news of the Pearl Harbor bombing? Or the assassination of John F. Kennedy? Or 9/11? (Substitute any other historical events that might apply.)

8. What would you consider the most important inventions during your lifetime?

9. Do you remember the first time you saw or used a television, a car, a refrigerator, a computer, the internet, a smartphone? (Substitute any others that apply.)

Harry and Evelyn (Billigmeier) Schott

In Their Footsteps

The Things You Don't Ask
(Original blog post: July 6, 2015)

I was always intrigued by the Salmon La Sac exit off Interstate 90. Partly because it's such a quirky name. But partly because, every time we drove by it on a family road trip, my mom used to say with nostalgia, "Oh, we used to go camping there."

Why did this comment never intrigue me enough to ask questions? Why did I never say in disbelief, "Camping? You went camping? Seriously?"

I don't think we ever went camping even once when I was a child. I vaguely remember visiting some cousins once when they were camping . . . and then I think we went to a motel. My mom never struck me as a "roughing it" sort of person. Neither of my parents did. So the fact that they camped at all should have sparked some interest.

Why did I never ask, "Why? What was so special about Salmon La Sac? Did you go there often?"

Last weekend, for the first time in my 54 years, I went to Salmon La Sac. It is a beautiful area, but no more beautiful than many other parts of the Cascade Mountains. Did my parents go there often so my mom's nostalgia came from familiarity? Did they go there with close friends and that made it meaningful? Did something special happen there? Was I conceived there? What?

Why did I never ask, "Who did you go camping with?"

My mom died seven years ago. My dad, nearly 40 years ago. I don't even know who I could ask now about why this was a special memory for my mom.

My hike at Salmon La Sac last weekend made me think of all the questions I should have asked my parents but never did. Or those I asked too late in life when my mother would brush off every question (especially the ones about how she and my dad dated, broke up, and then ended up married) with "That was so long ago. I don't remember."

What are all the things about my parents' lives that I should have found out more about, and now it's too late?

Maybe the Salmon La Sac story wasn't all that important. But maybe it would have revealed something about their pre-Carolyn life that would have helped me understand them better.

What else have I missed? Why didn't I ask more questions sooner?

Don't wait to ask the questions. Don't regret the things you never asked.

Travel Planning Checklist

Any travel requires at least a little bit of planning, even for the most spontaneous adventurers. And of course, some people are planners who like to have their whole trip planned from A to Z. Here's a checklist of items to consider when planning your travels. Some of these apply only to international travel.

- **Itinerary:** Choose your destination, and plan your trip itinerary.
- **Passport:** Make sure your passport is up-to-date and valid for at least six months after your trip (an entry requirement for some countries). Make a copy to take with you (and carry it separately from your actual passport to make it easy to replace if stolen) and a copy to leave at home or with a friend as an additional backup.
- **Visas:** Obtain visas, if needed, for any countries you're visiting.
- **Flight/hotels:** Make any necessary flight and hotel reservations. There are so many sites for booking flights and hotels (or B and Bs) that it's hard to recommend one, but I've listed some ideas in the next section.
- **Rail pass:** In many countries, getting around by train can be much simpler (and less expensive) than renting a car. In most cases, you'll buy train tickets at local stations during your travels. But if you'll be making extensive use of the train in Europe, for example, it may be worth it to buy a Eurail pass. These must be purchased ahead of time in the U.S. See www. eurail.com. (Note that other destinations also have rail passes, though I personally have less experience with these. The site, www.internationalrail.com, shows some of the options.)
- **Rental car:** Make rental car reservations, and check on insurance. Some credit card companies cover your insurance when renting a car, but there are lots of fine print and conditions. (Imagine my surprise when I found out Visa didn't cover my rental car insurance in the civilized first-world country of Ire-

land. Too many American tourists banging into the stone walls while driving down the left side of narrow Irish roads, I guess.)

- **International driver's license:** Obtain an international driver's license if you'll be renting a car. Although I almost always get one (from my local AAA office), I'll admit that I've rarely needed it in recent years as many countries don't require them. Still, if you're not sure, it's best to be prepared.

- **Money:** Throughout my travels, I rely on ATMs to get local currency and then use credit cards for those few big expenses. But I always carry some cash (divided into small amounts kept in different places in my luggage, purse, pockets) to get through the first 24 hours of the trip and to have a backup plan if a foreign ATM lets me down.

- **Credit cards:** Be sure to let your credit card company know you'll be using your card outside the country to avoid fraud alerts and having your card shut down. Also, check with your bank on the compatibility of your U.S. card with a chip outside of the country. Although most U.S. cards now have the chip, in some cases outside the U.S., you'll find that you still have to sign rather than use a PIN. I run into this more often with my credit card than with my ATM card. The website www.smartertravel.com has current information about what to consider and updates on current issues regarding obtaining money in other countries.

- **Family research:** Bring along your family research, maps, etc., both in electronic format on your laptop or tablet and a paper backup copy.

- **Local contacts:** If you've made local contacts or appointments, be sure to have their addresses and phone numbers so you can locate them or contact them if your plans change.

- **Other contacts:** It's helpful to make sure you have a list of emergency contacts (friends, your credit card company, travel insurance company, etc.) with you.

- **Travel insurance:** Buy travel insurance. I never used to bother with this, and then I broke my foot while traveling and started to think about the level of medical care in some places I've been and what I would have done if it had been a more serious accident. I've used World Nomads (www.worldnomads.com) because it was recommended by Lonely Planet, but there are many.
- **Cell phone:** Check with your cellular carrier about global roaming plans for the countries where you'll be traveling, and ask them about rates for voice, texting, and data. If you have an "unlocked" cell phone, one alternative when traveling overseas is to buy a local SIM card. A local SIM card means you'll have a different phone number each place you go, but it can save you money if you use your cell phone a lot

  Also, be very cautious about data usage, which can cause your phone bill to skyrocket. Talk to your cellular carrier about how to turn off and manage your data usage while traveling. The ins and outs of international cell phone usage change all the time, but www.smartertravel.com/international-cell-phone-guide usually has current information about the best options.
- **Prescriptions, glasses, etc.:** Be sure to have everything critical for your comfort and well-being with you (not in checked baggage), including a copy of any vital prescriptions.
- **Vaccinations:** Get any needed vaccinations. (Consult a travel health doctor or see wwwnc.cdc.gov/travel/destinations/list to determine what you need.)
- **Guidebook:** A good guidebook is worth its weight in gold, even though I do most of my planning using online resources.
- **Cloud storage:** Make copies of all your key documents (passport, insurance, family research, itinerary, etc.) and store them on Dropbox or any other cloud-based storage. If key documents are stolen, or you just have a ton of family research

documents and photos that you don't want to carry with you, having them accessible via the cloud can save your sanity.

- **Duct tape:** Don't laugh. I can't tell you how many times I've found a good use for duct tape. Well, yes, I can tell you. Read on.

Strategic use of duct tape

In Their Footsteps

Duct Tape: Don't Leave Home Without It
(Original blog post: May 2, 2010)

My flirtation with duct tape as an indispensable travel accessory started in Ireland. I was at the beginning of a two-month trip through Europe when my favorite hair conditioner tube sprung a leak.

While I knew this was somewhat less than a tragedy, I still didn't want two months of bad hair days from using a strange replacement brand. So I roamed through the local hardware store in An Daingean for a solution and came back to the hotel with a roll of duct tape. Sure enough, that sealed the tube so it lasted the entire two months of the trip and for another couple months after I got home.

At first, I only used duct tape in fairly predictable ways, such as repairing a tear in my suitcase until I could get it home to be fixed. But breaking my foot spurred my creativity.

The hospital in Croatia had given me a "cast" that was mostly gauze wrapped around a little bit of plaster. When the gauze frayed too much, I was told "just come back, and we'll wrap it again."

That didn't give me great confidence about how well it would stand up while I traveled. But a little duct tape applied to the bottom of my foot kept the gauze from fraying as I tromped through parking lots and airports toward an upgraded cast. From then on, duct tape became the first solution I thought of for almost any problem, such as:

- To seal an open wine bottle overnight when the cork wouldn't go back in.
- To hold together a bulging box and keep Turkish Delight from spilling throughout my suitcase.
- To hold a hanger in front of an open window so I could air out my sweater, which reeked after I sat in a smoky internet café.
- To mark a friend's suitcase, which I was carrying home for her, so I could recognize it among all the other nondescript black suitcases in the baggage claim.

And the most strategic use of all was to keep a friend's toilet tank from leaking after it cracked during a holiday weekend in Moldova. Duct tape kept the toilet functional until the repairman could get there a few days later.

Neck pillows and travel clotheslines and TSA-approved luggage locks are all fine. But for me, the first thing to be packed for any trip is duct tape!

Travel Planning Resources

Online travel resources

Doing an internet search for the name of the place you're going will likely yield more websites than you can look at. Try combining the place name with "tourism" or "history" or "archives" or "museum" to get a more focused set of results for what you'd like to see in your ancestral town or the area.

Each of the guidebook series listed below also has a website with travel information, blogs, and discussion boards. These discussion boards are especially useful because travelers using a guidebook you like will probably have a similar outlook on travel as you do, making their feedback especially relevant to your needs.

Some other websites that give feedback from actual travelers are www.tripadvisor.com and www.yahoo.com/travel. One caution about relying on feedback from these sites is that you don't know if the person commenting has tastes or expectations similar to your own. I read one review that was very critical of an Eastern European hotel. From the comments, it was apparent this person expected American-style accommodations, which was unrealistic in that region unless you stay at a Hilton or Sheraton or one of the other big-name hotels. I knew this; the reviewer apparently didn't. (They complained about the very things I thought added to the charm of the place.) Since their expectations differed from mine, their comments were not useful to me.

Another site to explore is www.wikitravel.org. Similar in concept to Wikipedia, the information is provided by people with an interest in a specific geographical area. It lists sights, hotels, restaurants, transportation, and internet cafés.

Transportation

You'll need to arrange transportation from home to your main destination. If that's an airline, you can book your travel either online or through a traditional travel agent. Online travel options are constantly changing, but some good websites for flights are www.kayak.com, www.expedia.com, and www.orbitz.com. I've also had good luck with www.whichbudget.com for flights within Europe (although this site also covers travel to other destinations).

You'll also need to arrange transportation within your destination area to your ancestral town. Depending on the local situation and your comfort level, this may be a rental car, train, bus, boat, or taxi. I usually like to rent a car because it gives me the most flexibility. But that may not make sense if it's a destination where you're not comfortable driving. In that case, I'd probably use the train, public transportation like a bus or marshrutka (a minibus that is common in Eastern Europe), or in some cases, hire a car and driver. (That sounds extravagant, but it is actually a very practical alternative in some places.)

To help you plan your trip, up-to-date schedule information for trains, long-distance buses, and boats is available online or through a travel guidebook. This can help you decide on routes and transportation alternatives. For example, I didn't want to rent a car and drive in Croatia and Bosnia, but when I saw the complexity of the train, ferry, and bus connections, I realized a car was my only option without completely changing my itinerary.

Also consider local conditions. Even though I'm a reasonably independent traveler, I've always hired a driver in Ukraine and Moldova because the roads in rural areas are unbelievably bad, signposts are nonexistent, and border crossings in Moldova are problematic. There are often local police who stop you to get a bribe (which happened twice on my last trip there). Fortunately, with Vova, our knowledgeable driver, at the wheel, this was handled with no problem and actually became part of the adventure. My cousin Justin has also successfully used marshrutkas to travel to ancestral towns in Ukraine and Moldova.

Hotels

You may want to reserve rooms in advance, or you may just play it by ear. (Personally, I like to have a hotel reservation when I fly into a country or if I arrive somewhere late at night, even if I'm more spontaneous the rest of the trip.) I've had good luck with www.booking.com and www.airbnb.com for hotel reservations. A guidebook can also provide suggestions for you.

If you're traveling during a high tourist season, you may want to reserve in advance to prevent the uncertainty of having to hunt for a room or the dubious adventure of ending up in a fleabag place. On one spontaneously decided overnight stay in London, I ended up in a hotel in which I suspect the other guests were paying by the hour. I couldn't get out of there fast enough the next morning.

I generally like to be as spontaneous as possible. But on one trip, I realized with all the appointments I'd made, I was tied to a schedule that didn't allow for much spontaneity. So it made sense to book everything in advance rather than spend time looking for a hotel in each location. If you're only going to be somewhere a short time, you may not want to waste your precious time there searching for a hotel.

Guidebooks

Although I do most of my planning online these days, a good travel guidebook, written within the last year or so, still goes with me to most destinations as they can give detailed information about planning the basic logistics and all the ins and outs of finding transportation in specific locations. I would advise picking a guidebook that fits your personality and travel style, then follow the suggestions there. Each guidebook series targets different types of travelers, with different budgets and travel expectations.

Of course, if you're traveling to an ancestral town, there's a good chance you'll be off the beaten path in a location that no guidebooks mention. However, you may prefer to find a hotel in a nearby larger town covered by a guidebook and visit your ancestral town and other sights from that base.

My own favorite series for European travel is the Rick Steves' guidebooks. The philosophy of this series is to "travel like a temporary local." They are written in a lively and humorous way. They do a great job of highlighting the most interesting sights (and are blunt about telling you when a famous sight is not actually that interesting). They also have very good insights about the country and its culture and people, as well as practical information on everything from transportation to where to do laundry.

I think Rick does a good job of covering a wide range of accommodation choices, from very nice hotels to hostels, with a focus on clean midrange hotels. (Although one college-age traveler I talked to in Slovenia told me his suggestions were all too upscale and expensive for her, despite his hostel listings.)

Guidebooks are available that cover Europe, Asia, North and South America, Australia, Africa, the Caribbean, etc. Some of the major guidebook series are Lonely Planet (my personal first choice for locations not covered by Rick Steves), Fodor's, Frommer's, Bradt, Let's Go, Access, and Rough Guides. Each of these has its own style and focus, which vary from targeting upscale travelers to backpackers; from popular destinations to remote ones; from classic sights (the Eiffel Tower in Paris) to lesser known attractions (the Museum of Oil in Ploieşti, Romania).

Lonely Planet guidebooks cover low- to moderate-priced accommodations and are thorough and well-researched with lots of maps. They're informal but informative in their descriptions and can be blunt, for example, when something is a rip-off.

The Fodor's and Frommer's series both tend to focus on more upscale travel. Their hotel suggestions are generally more expensive and Americanized; the sights they review are more traditional. Frommer's has some good information on family-friendly hotels and sights.

Rough Guides guidebooks use contemporary language and include good, detailed information, although I know people who have used this series and report that information is not always easy to find quickly. These guidebooks focus on low-budget travel and less mainstream sightseeing options. The Let's Go guidebooks have a similar focus to Rough Guides.

The Bradt guidebooks cover more unusual destinations and are champions of sustainable travel, with a decent amount of practical information and a range of accommodation choices.

The Access guidebooks focus on cities and organize their information by neighborhood. This series may not be useful to you unless you're staying in a city while doing day trips to your ancestral towns.

Look for the guidebook that best suits your style of travel because hotel, transportation, and even sightseeing recommendations are geared toward its typical audience.

For the U.S., another option is the AAA guidebooks, free with AAA membership. They do a good job of thoroughly covering accommodations, even in smaller towns, which can be useful on a family history trip. Some of the travel guide series mentioned above also cover the U.S. and Canada.

Many of these guidebooks are available in e-book formats. This can give you the option of taking several with you without carrying multiple bulky guidebooks. However, e-book readers may not show maps and other illustrations well, so you may want to consider how important those are to you.

In Their Footsteps

Nine Tips for Traveling Where You Don't Speak the Language
(Original blog post: November 19, 2014)

"I don't speak the language" seems to be the most often expressed fear people have about traveling to another country. But to me, that's always seemed a very limiting way to look at travel. Most of us don't speak more than one or two languages, so if you restrict yourself to countries where those languages are spoken, you're missing out on a lot of the world.

Visiting a country where you're a linguistic idiot may mean that you won't be able to have a deep conversation with the locals about global politics, but that doesn't mean you need to avoid these places. Here are a few simple ideas of how to get around.

1. Learn a few words/key phrases.

Before you go, learn some key phrases. I think the most important phrase to learn is "I don't understand." This was by far the phrase I used most often when I recently spent two weeks in Ukraine. My badly pronounced *"Ya nay penyamayo"* invariably caused the person speaking to me to smile, but they walked away to find someone else who could help them.

It's also good to learn some basic pleasantries: Hello, good-bye, excuse me, thank you, please. And a couple of key questions words, such as "how much" and "where," are always useful. Don't worry too much about language elegance. "Where metro?" is a bit abrupt, but it communicated my need just as effectively as "Can you help me find the nearest metro station?"—and it was a lot easier to learn and remember.

2. Learn the alphabet.

If you're going somewhere that uses an alphabet that you don't know, take a little time to learn how the letters sound. Even if you don't understand the language itself, there's great comfort in being able to sound out something on a menu and realize that десерт is dessert.

This is also helpful in reading street signs. I might still be driving around Greece lost if I hadn't known that Δελφοί on the road signs was directing me to Delphi.

3. Let your inner actor loose.

Don't be shy; be willing to look a little silly and act out what you're trying to say. The server in the restaurant or a new local friend may not understand "Your cooking is just like my mom's. That dinner was delicious!" But if you act out eating (hold an imaginary fork and shovel food in your mouth), then give a big smile and say "Mmmm!" they'll know what you're trying to say. Or if you hold up three fingers in addition to saying in English "I'd like three metro tokens," you're much more likely to get what you want with minimum confusion.

If you're shy about charades, carry pencil and paper with you so you can draw a picture of what you mean or write out numbers (especially useful in asking the cost of something you want to buy).

4. Watch body language.

You may not understand every word (or any words), but watching the body language of someone speaking another language often helps you puzzle out the gist of what they're saying. When I was in Ukraine as an international election observer, I only understood four words of what the angry Russian man said to me. But his body language (in my face, angry voice and arm movements) made it clear that he didn't appreciate the interference of Americans and that I needed to move away from him.

5. Scope out difficult situations in advance.

If you're going to do something complex that requires decisions, try to gather information in advance about the options. You may be able to do this on the internet or with English-speaking hotel staff or an English-speaking acquaintance. If you know in advance that, when buying a train ticket, you'll be asked to decide on options like *asiento reservado* (reserved seat) or *tren rápido* (express train), your conversation with the ticket seller in the Madrid train station is more likely to go smoothly.

6. Remember that volume doesn't equal translation.

If you speak English (or Spanish or Mandarin), you're in luck because these are the most commonly spoken languages in the world. So you're likely to encounter someone in your travels who speaks your native language and can help you.

Of course, it's likely that they won't speak your native language as well as you do, and they may have trouble understanding what you're saying. In those situations, speak more slowly, but not more loudly. Yelling something at a stranger in English will not improve their English skills. It will only make you sound annoying. Or imply that you think they're deaf.

Speak slowly, enunciate, and use simple, commonly used words to make it easy for them to understand you.

7. Translate key phrases ahead of time.

There may be situations where it's important to communicate something complex more exactly. When I visited my ancestral towns in Poland, I needed to be able to communicate that my ancestors had come from that village and that I was looking for the old German cemetery and church. This is difficult to act out no matter how good of an actor you are.

For this situation, I wrote out my questions ahead of time and used Google to translate them to Polish. When I encountered people in these villages, I handed them a piece of paper with my translated questions. I still had to understand their responses, but most of my questions were yes/no questions or allowed them to literally point me in the right direction.

8. Use technology.

Smartphones and Wi-Fi are your friends. If you have access to the internet, using Google Translate is an easy way to get quick translations for words or simple phrases when you're talking with someone in another language. If you're not sure you'll have internet access, download a stand-alone translation app that doesn't need the internet.

9. Relax.

I confess that after a few shots of vodka, I was relaxed enough that it didn't matter that my hosts Larisa and Sergio didn't speak much English. Somehow their Russian seemed more understandable, and they seemed to understand my English better. (Of course, it helped that my friends Jim and Marianna were able to translate some of what they were saying.) Alcohol may or may not be your thing—but it certainly seems to help one relax and to make conversation flow better!

Acknowledgements

As I've been on my journey of researching my family history and traveling to my own ancestral towns, there have been many people who have inspired me, helped me, and made the journey special. Family members, genealogy buddies, fellow travelers, guides, and new-found friends: you are too numerous to name, but I so appreciate each of you!

My special thanks to friends who have allowed me to share their stories and photos in this book: Gayla and Rich Aspenleiter, Valya and Milt Kramer, Elaine Morrison, Bob Schneider, Elli Wise, Justin Ehresman, Meatra Keo, Amanda Dahmes. And I am so grateful to those who have guided me on my visits to ancestral villages in Ukraine: Serge Yelizarov, Peter, Karolina Fromm, Inna Stryukova, Bob Schneider.

I'd also like to acknowledge my editors, Kathy Burge and Jennie Gulian, who helped me find the right words and polish my existing words through three editions. For the third edition, I wanted a different look for the cover, and Matthew Ip delivered with a fresh, new cover design—thank you!

Carolyn Schott
Seattle, Washington
January 2019

About the Author

Carolyn Schott has been a lifelong traveler, with a special interest in exploring places related to her heritage. This has taken her to Germany, Ukraine, Moldova, Hungary, and Poland. Along the way, she's sampled *Zwiebelkuchen* (onion tart) at a German village festival; celebrated Easter in Moldova; hiked through rural cemeteries with a broken foot; found herself in a protest in Kyiv, Ukraine; and learned to appreciate the bonding powers of a good vodka.

Carolyn has more than 20 years of genealogy experience. She's one of the founders of the Black Sea German Research group (blackseagr.org), and formerly a board member of the Germans from Russia Heritage Society (GRHS) and editor of the GRHS *Heritage Review*. Her writing has received several awards from the International Society of Family History Writers and Editors, and she is a regular speaker on genealogy-related topics.